Praying Your Child Through Anything

Real Stories, Real Prayers, Real Peace

By Beth Leonard

Copyright 2020 by Beth Leonard

ISBN: 978-0-578-79876-9

Scripture texts in this work are taken from the *New American Bible, revised edition* © 2010, 1991, 1986, 1970 Confraternity of Christian Doctrine, Washington, D.C. and are used by permission of the copyright owner. All Rights Reserved. No part of the New American Bible may be reproduced in any form without permission in writing from the copyright owner.

Dedication

To my husband, Bill: I wouldn't have wanted to parent with anyone else. You are incredible.

To my daughters, Sarah and Moira: I love and respect your beautiful souls. It is my greatest honor in life to be your mom and always know that I will never stop praying for you.

To my grandson, Cayden: I love you to the moon and back. Be a good boy and hold tight to your rosary. It is your weapon!

To my mom and dad, Loretta and Ron Caffoe: The best parents a girl could dream of. R.I.P dear dad and keep praying for us in heaven.

Acknowledgments

To all the parents who made this book possible by sharing their incredible stories of prayer, love and hope for their children.

A very special thank you to Christine Moss, my dear friend in Christ Jesus, for all the hours she spent reading, correcting and fine-tuning every paragraph. I call her my Spiritual Editor because every time we sat down to review her notes, she started us in prayer to the Holy Spirit. Her suggestions were always spot-on as she continued to encourage me to complete the manuscript.

Special thanks to the book's editor, Ellen Hrkach, who had the vision I was desperately lacking in how to layout the stories and prayers to be crisp, concise and polished. She is an amazing lady who is always willing to share her love for books and writing to inspire others along their journey. Ellen is an award-winning Author, Editor, Publisher, Book Coach, NFP Teacher and Speaker. I thank her from the bottom of my heart. Ellen Gable Hrkach, ellengable.wordpress.com

Book Cover thanks goes to my artistically dear friend who knows me so well through our many hours of fellowship and prayer that all I had to do was tell her the book title and she immediately had a cover photo in mind… utilizing my own daughter and grandson. Jennifer doesn't just take photos, she captures memories, feelings and moments in time that will joyfully dance within our hearts and minds for generations to come. Jennifer Driscoll Photography, photosbyjennifer.com and photosbyjen on Instagram.

Table of Contents

Introduction and Prayer for all Parents	1
Praying Your Child Through Anything…	
Even when a mental illness requires desperate measures	6
Even a life-threatening eating disorder	12
Even depression and self-harm	18
Even when your rebellious teen challenges your patience	29
Even when your child chooses to struggle alone	39
Even when he announces his same-sex attraction	46
Even the sudden death of a beloved father	52
Even a severely impaired mind and body	60
Even a most humbling miracle	65
Even a call to the priesthood	71
Even from lost to leader	81
Even the walk home to be with God	92
Even an addiction to heroin	104
Afterword, Author's note	
About the Author	112

Introduction

Over the past five years, I have had the pleasure to meet some extraordinary parents who prayed their children through some incredible circumstances. Hearing their stories intrigued me and piqued my curiosity for more. I desired to understand how parents cope when faced with unique and uncharted challenges, what inspires them to persevere, from where do they draw strength, and finally... I truly wanted to know what their prayer sounded like when it left Earth and rose up to Heaven.

In this book, you will meet humble parents who have one thing in common: they pray! Yes, they pray their children through the good times and bad, the serious doubt and the remarkable revelations, the exhilarating joys and the heartbreaking sorrows, the turmoil of the unknown and the calmness of faith, and even the fearful retreats and brave moves forward. They literally pray their children through everything and anything, and you are about to hear their most intimate encounters with the Almighty God who delivered them through it.

Before we get into the heart of the book, perhaps we should pay tribute to all parents who, for thousands of years, have raised and prayed for their children. Children become parents, parents become grandparents, grandparents become great-grandparents, etc. The prayers never stop--weaving webs of holy security through entire family trees, linking to and overlapping with other branches and family trees. This worldwide web, pun intended, can be viewed as a network of prayer, connecting this Earth to the celestial heavens. Generation after generation exists because God continues to co-create with humans, bringing bundles of joy to families across the globe.

The Holy Bible tells us that Adam and Eve started us off in the Old Testament and Joseph and Mary in the New Testament. God chooses to mark His world-changing occasions in a special way. It is not through huge fanfare, a party, or a thunderbolt that lights up the sky. It is with something He values as most dear and necessary.

God's messages of hope and love for all of mankind always begin with… parents.

How It All Began

Before I formed you in the womb I knew you,/ before you were born I dedicated you,/ a prophet to the nations I appointed you. Jeremiah 1:5

God forms unique and unrepeatable souls and sends each of us to Earth to carry out our mission. He remains eager for our return to Him upon the completion of our tasks, as His promised inheritance awaits our heavenly arrival. He desires for each of us to call upon Him daily for guidance and to use the gifts He has given us to help ourselves and those around us. He is proud of each of us, His creations, and knows the world is in need of our presence.

To give each new life the best possible chance of survival, He awards parents with the task at hand. As a parent, you are to be loving as you guide and teach your child all the days of your life. And most importantly, He awaits your call for guidance. He listens intently to hear the words He longs for and the request that will bring you closer to His heart as you begin… praying your child through anything.

The following are two prayers for those mothers and fathers who are just now beginning the process of praying for their children.

A Prayer for a Mother Struggling to Conceive

Dear Abba Father,

You are the Creator of all. Your masterpieces are found all over the world and throughout the universe. The human being, brought forth out of love and designed in Your own likeness and image, is one of Your finest works. I yearn to be filled with Your love and to feel that love in a special way throughout my body. I ache for the fullness of a child placed within my womb. I yearn to be blessed by You in this way.

Please consider my plea and know that we desire, with your guidance, to be holy parents. We will begin this day and each day hereafter praying for the soul You will create for us.

We pray for patience to endure the wait and understand if our request is not Your will. If the biological door shall remain closed to us, please lead us through the window of parenthood and reveal to us the ways we can fill this yearning desire. Please open and soften our hearts and minds to the needs around us so as not to overlook any invitation You send our way. Prepare us daily, Dear Lord, for whatever task you have planned for us. We explicitly trust You as we await Your perfect timing and anticipate the many joys You will bring forth. Amen.

A Prayer for the Baby in the Womb

Dear Almighty One,

I imagine the face of the child within my womb, the same child You have already held as You blew life into the soul. You formed and knit this child together with a one-of-a-kind pattern You will never create again. Within me is a brand new and unique creation, a flower that has never been seen before. I am eager to meet this child and to hold and cradle the little one in my arms. I imagine the birth of Jesus, Your Son, as He so humbly entered this world. Warmer and safer in his mother's womb, still He was drawn out into the coldness of the world He would save.

I pray for the two hands of my babe, that they may serve You in prayer, give to the needy and graciously accept what is given to them. I pray for strong legs to endure the earthly crosses, run to the aid of others and firmly stand for what is right. I pray for their tiny ears to hear Your call, sweet lips to proclaim Your glory, and caring eyes to see Your great wonders. I pray for their heart and mind, that they know You and will experience the fullness of Your abundant love and endless mercy. I pray for their soul, its sanctification, and eventually its return to You in Heaven for eternity.

As the child continues to grow and mature inside me, help me use these valuable days, weeks and months to grow also—in wisdom, understanding, love and faith. Teach me, wise Father, of the things I am to know to be a holy mother to this precious gift within me. I nest my soul within Your Mighty branches, and I am open to Your guidance like a baby bird to its mother. Teach me to open my eyes to Your truths within the world. Shelter me and be my refuge by day and night. Sing me songs of love so I will know Your voice. Feed me daily with the bread that nourishes me so I can grow stronger. Place Your Word within me that it should be our sweet language of hope and perseverance. Prepare me for this child, dear Lord… and when I am ready, help me to fly. Amen.

Prayer Prompt

Read the story of the Prodigal Son (Luke 15:11-32) three times. One time as if you were the noble son, one time as the prodigal son and one time as the father. Considering our entire life, we most likely can relate, in some way, to each of their sides. Listen for the different lessons it teaches and the messages it offers us for how to understand each other's perspectives.

Meditation Prayer for a Parent of a Child of Any Age

Dear Father,

There is no other gift more precious than the soul of a human life, as each of us are fashioned in the likeness and image of our Creator, God. Every soul, claimed by You, will have eternal life. Therefore, dear Lord, I joyfully embrace the blessing of [name], the child you have created for me. In return for Your generosity, I ask that You accept my prayers for [his/her] eternal salvation.

Please, dear Father, I offer:

Thanksgiving... to lift up my child
Concern... to cover [him/her] with safety
Love... that [he/she] will always know it surrounds [him/her]

I ask for these blessings upon my child as I pray for:

Friendships... that [name] may choose wisely
Strength... to battle evil
Discernment... that [he/she] be led not astray
Humility... so [he/she] may find rest and peace in You rather than the world. Amen.

Praying Your Child Through Anything
...Even When a Mental Illness
Requires Desperate Measures

The God of all grace who called you to his eternal glory through Christ [Jesus] will himself restore, confirm, strengthen, and establish you after you have suffered a little. To him be dominion forever, Amen. 1 Peter 5:10-11

Sitting down to talk with Jeanne about her daughter, Laurie, was like entering the classroom of a saint. When I arrived at her home, she had a small feast of delicious homemade cookies and desserts on a table and promptly brought me my choice of tea or coffee in the daintiest china cup. She truly is an extraordinary woman who, now in her late 80s, still wakes early to attend daily 8:00 a.m. Mass. She loves Jesus and Jesus loves her back. You know He does because you can see Him living in her devoted eyes, you can feel His presence in her accepting manner, and you can hear Him speak through her soft yet passionate words.

The story that brought me to her home happened over 50 ago, when she was but a young mom with five children in tow. After spending time with Jeanne, I now believe she alone could have supplied me with enough prayers to fill an entire book. Her life has not been an easy one, filled with many sorrows and suffering, but God has always pulled her through. She has prayed her children, and now their families, through everything and anything. She proclaims, "God cannot be outdone in generosity" and has many testimonies to prove it. Laurie, Jeanne's daughter, was the recipient of one of God's most generous gifts.

Seeking the Doctor's Advice

Jeanne Atkins was ready to move her family of seven from Virginia back to their home state of Indiana as they followed her husband's career. Before they rolled out of town, they had one issue that must be dealt with; the deteriorating mental health of their daughter, Laurie. It all started gradually but had since escalated to a very worrisome state. Laurie was experiencing the onset of a series of deeply depressive moods and frightening isolated behaviors. It was as if Laurie had sealed herself inside an invisible sound-proof box; she was often unaware of her surroundings, and Jeanne and her husband were unable to comfort her.

On the advice of her doctor, Jeanne took her daughter Laurie to a highly regarded psychiatrist. Eager to hear his assessment, Jeanne sat patiently as all the data was taken into consideration. The verdict: Laurie was to be immediately institutionalized. Her only hope was to be guarded 24 hours a day, seven days a week, by a highly trained medical team who would try to reach her. Jeanne thought for only a moment before saying that his recommendation would not be possible since they were planning a move. Jeanne was horrified at the thought of handing her daughter over to complete strangers and then abandoning her by moving several states away.

The doctor countered her objection by telling her that Laurie most likely would not even make it through the trip. He feared she was dangerous to herself and that her moods could not be trusted. His biggest fear of traveling at length with her was that she would simply open the car door and slip out to her death.

Jeanne informed him that there was absolutely no chance of that. She had just purchased a new Lincoln Continental and had noticed the doors in the back seat could not be opened from the inside. Providentially, she had not made it back to the dealership to have it fixed, so she would just leave the car "broken" until after the trip. (Yes, Jeanne later found that her problem had an easy fix, and actually, the new feature was called "child lock"!)

The doctor's professional counsel remained steadfast and his concern for them leaving his office without heeding his instruction was troubling to him. He once again warned her as she got up to leave. To that, she distinctly remembers saying, "So what you are saying to me is that I only have God." As she turned to open the door, she remembers a confidence filled her, and she thought to herself, *how strange I would say I **only** have God. If I have God, I have everything.*

Seeking God's Advice

Jeanne knew the problem at hand was serious, and she knew that it could not be ignored. She pondered what to do and decided to offer a 40-day fast* and prayer in return for heavenly guidance, as it would be necessary for her to eventually make tough decisions about her daughter's well-being. Guided by the example of Jesus, she knew that fasting and prayer were important to Jesus when he sought strength and guidance from God, His Father. She, too, was seeking life-changing answers and found comfort that she was on the right path as she followed the footsteps of Jesus into the desert.

For forty days, Jeanne ate only bread and drank only water, yet she continued to cook for and feed her five children and her husband. She prayed the Rosary, attended Mass and prayed for help. When I asked Jeanne what her children thought of her not eating with them, she said she didn't think they really noticed. She sat with them and kept herself busy with the youngest children. She was not a person to show or impose her suffering—she just did it with humility.

At the end of the forty days, she looked to God for the direction she sought. She asked God to guide them to the best doctors for Laurie's on-going care and for the wisdom to know what she could do to best hold onto the daughter that was quickly slipping away. The answer came in the form of a clear and unmistakable command. It was not the answer she expected, not even one she would have ever considered.

Fasting and Prayer Answered

The voice rewarded the prayer, the fasting and the patience with these simple words, "take her off all of her medications." Laurie had been on a few important medications for years, and certainly way before any of the problems had manifested. Seeking confirmation and support to follow this heavenly inspiration, she placed a call to her husband. His response was firm; there would be no taking her off the medication. He feared that taking her off these medications would only add to her misery. Jeanne remembers her reaction was very calm and submissive to the husband she loved and highly regarded. She sided with her husband because that is the kind of woman she is.

God rewarded her fidelity by changing the heart of her husband, Tom. Within ten minutes of hanging up, her husband called back. Tom had reconsidered his abrupt decision and softened to the thought that there may be more to this gift from God. He recalled how devoted his wife was to her children, the solemn request she took to prayer, and the fasting for forty days that she had endured. With those thoughts, and most likely a prompting from the Holy Spirit, Tom agreed that they should heed the direction she was given.

Miraculously, within days of stopping the medications, Laurie was free from all of the emotional and mental anguish she had experienced for years. Much later, Jeanne and Tom discovered that others in the extended family were highly allergic to an assortment of over-the-counter and prescription medications. An undetected allergy could have been the cause of Laurie's mental and emotional changes as she grew from childhood through her adolescence.

A Plea to the Divine Physician

Dear Divine Physician, sometimes I find it difficult to distinguish what is best for my child. How do I know when You are speaking through the so-called experts of the world and when You are in direct opposition to their guidance? Is it through my own sacrifice, prayer and willingness to listen that You will answer me? Please, dear Lord, open my body, mind and soul to Your direction. Accept my sacrifices, prayers and offerings for the child that You and I love.

My fast of forty days I offer, along with my prayers and devotion to You. This fast is my promise to You, in hopes that Your mercy might give me the grace of Your reply. I ask You to strengthen me as You once strengthened Jesus during His fast in the desert and again during His Agony in the Garden. I need only You to lean on. With all my weight, I am casting my life into Your mighty arms.

I come before You because You are our Creator. You lovingly formed Laurie, knit her together, and placed her within my womb. Your eyes never part from her, and You know every detail of her being. I love this child, and my heart is heavy as she struggles. Your beautiful creation has morphed from happiness and smiles to misery and hollow glares. Only you, Almighty Physician, could know where the danger lies within her.

I trust in Your Almighty Providence and know that I am nothing without You. Please bring peace back to Laurie, our daughter. Placing all of my trust in Your wisdom as I pray through Christ our Lord, Amen.

This prayer was inspired by the interview with:
Jeanne Atkins, Founder of Atkins Cheesecakes and Fine Desserts.

Jeanne would like to dedicate this story to the repose of the soul of Laurie Atkins Strand and her loving family. Laurie died from breast cancer at the age of 52, survived by her husband, son and two daughters.

---

* Forty-Day Fast—Like Jesus' fast for forty days in the desert (cf, Matthew 4 and Luke 4), fasting is a prayer and sacrifice tradition used to bring the faithful closer to God, especially during Lent or in times of need for deeper and focused prayer. Fasting takes on many forms and can even be a short half-day or one day fast. It also can be a fast from something you normally do to pass the time at home or in the car (like watching television or listening to music) and opening yourself up to prayer, discernment and listening. It is believed that depriving ourselves of something we normally do causes us to be a bit "uncomfortable." This uncomfortable feeling is used to redirect our attention, thoughts and actions toward God when we allow the emptiness and awkwardness of silence to be filled with God's graces and mercy.

Prayer Prompt

Jesus is the Divine Physician who healed many throughout his earthly ministry, but Jesus has never stopped healing us. His healing hands remain at work throughout the world— in a mother's touch, a dear friend's warm embrace, a surgeon's skill, a teacher's insight, a chemist's find, a pastor's blessing, and a caregiver's gentle way. Feel His presence and His calming touch before you pray.

Meditation Prayer for Children With a Mental Illness Requiring Desperate Measures

I come to you with a broken heart for the child who seems so distant, even though [he/she] sits not but a room away from me. Please accept my humble sacrifice [name the sacrifice] in exchange for a way to reach [name], so that with Your heavenly assistance, I may be a guide through this terrifying maze. Please hear my desperate prayer for the beloved child whom You entrusted to my earthly care.

Melt away the walls that separate us and be the conduit between us. I beg You to reach with one almighty hand into the soul of [name] and, with the other hand, extend it into my own soul. Then, dear Lord, through the radiance of Your loving heart, may we once again be united. Through You, all things are possible.

You are the Prince of Peace, and I shall use Your peace as my compass, keeping me on track so I do not stray from Your calming voice and sound advice. Send Your peace to lace the rugged trail of struggles chosen for [name] and me. Oh, my Savior and wonderous God, I will follow You wherever You lead. Please hear and answer me. Amen.

Praying Your Child Through Anything
...Even a Life-Threatening Eating Disorder

"Trusting all your affairs to Him and putting them also under the protection of Mary and Joseph, you will see that all will be well." (St. Theodore Guerin)

As ironic as it may seem, I met the funniest guy I have ever known while on a Catholic pilgrimage to New York City. His gift, and actual job for decades, is making people laugh. Tom Leopold finds the brighter side of every situation and uses his gift to melt away the tensions of life. I can honestly say that my sides hurt from continuous laughing every day of our pilgrimage.

As for his wife, Barbara, she is one very beautiful lady with a sweet disposition who is visibly enamored with Tom's swift humor. She smiles and laughs along with all of us, whether or not she has heard the quip before. They are a delight to share time with, and I found conversation to be effortless while sitting down to dinner beside the amusing couple.

We spoke about many things, one of which was about my writing this book. I noticed the shields of carefree humor seemingly drift away as they told me of their very own precious recipient of numerous prayers. For years, their daughter had been suffering from a life-threatening eating disorder. It was one that initially was passed off as a phase, only later to be recognized for the devastation it had caused within her body— physically, spiritually and emotionally.

Early Signs

With anorexia, the early signs are hardly noticeable. She might pass on a few family meals, but the excuses seem reasonable. Teenagers can easily cover their tracks with statements like: "I ate a huge lunch today," or "I'll grab something later," or "so-and-so's mom fed us dinner when I was at her house after school." Even if parents notice something askew, it is easy to assume everything will soon return to normal. There is no need to sound an alarm over a few missed meals! But when excuses persist and begin challenging the parents' intuition, a more watchful eye is called for.

They noticed their daughter became increasingly obsessed with the way she looked and her body weight. She was pre-occupied with the food she ate, and family dinners at restaurants sent her into a high anxiety mode, causing her to make up any excuse to leave. Signs of purging became more evident, and she wore layers of clothing to hide her secret. What began disguised as a new lifestyle of healthy choices ended up a nearly irreversible obsession with harmful self-control and dangerous withdrawal.

Escalated Concerns

Tom said his concerns were validated one evening as they sat in a Radio City Music Hall theatre enjoying the Christmas Spectacular show. Happy to be sharing this family tradition with his wife and two daughters, he put his arm around the daughter sitting closest to him. Tom remembers her leaning into him for a sweet father-daughter hug, when he noticed her shocking frailness. Loose-fitting clothes can hide secrets from the eyes, but a touch is true and all-knowing.

Aching from his new discovery, Tom turned his attention back to the stage as the Nativity scene came to life, and one bright star hovered over the stable. Humble shepherds with live animals came to adore the baby, angelic voices sang hymns of praise, ornate costumes graced the now-packed stage, and three glorious and sparkling kings were set to offer their gifts. Yet, with all the fanfare to behold, he remembers feeling drawn in, as never before, to the humble mother of Jesus. Softly he whispered to Mary that somehow, just now, he was painfully awakened to the suffering she would endure during her life as the mother of Jesus. He both recognized her intense joy at the birth of her son but also felt her great sorrow during his crucifixion. He found an odd connection to her and believes it was a grace, a sort of unified blessing, that allowed him to join in Mary's sorrows, which would help sustain him through his own sufferings yet to come. It was the first of many tangible gifts of comfort he would receive as he opened the door to a new and uncertain life. He knew, during that special moment, that it was time to get involved, ask the necessary questions, and begin an attack on the demon-like disease called anorexia that was devouring his daughter.

The Battle Is On

Tom and Barbara fought beside their daughter to turn the tide in her favor, and they solicited the help of many, including both local and remote professionals and medical care teams. They were concerned about her physical body because of the starvation, inherent with anorexia, which can take a toll on the heart and other essential organs. Her mental state was also in jeopardy, as the disease often plays mind-games and heaps on depression. And then there was the spiritual side, where she perceived that the disease robbed her of who she was in the eyes of God and viciously attacked her self-worth. Seeking help and the right weapons to fight the disease would be a routine they would continue, off and on, for many years.

Peace

As we talked, they maintained concern on their faces, but it was a healthy kind. Perhaps it is best to say that it was a peaceful kind of disquiet, if that makes any sense. Imagine firefighters seemingly at ease at the station dinner table. They are laughing and enjoying the food, but a closer look reveals what lies just beneath the tabletop and the t-shirts they wear. Their flame-resistant brush pants are on, their boots are laced up, and their unzipped jackets hang on the back of their chairs— as they are always ready if the alarm should ring.

That is how parents learn to live their lives when a child is teetering between life and death. The illness is relentless, and it takes every weapon she has to keep the monster quiet. But the monster works overtime and looks for any new vulnerabilities it can exploit in hopes she will once again succumb to its power.

Yes, the concern for calamity opens each new day but so does peace, through prayer, as it pours out in equal or greater measure to anxiousness or worry. It is Tom and Barbara's faith in Christ that daily leads them through the pain, suffering and struggles inherent in loving a child through a life-threatening eating disorder.

Lord, Please Help Me For I Am Lost

Dear Lord,

There is no ache that compares to the ache I am feeling right now. Are these not the years carved out for parents to "fight" with daughters over things like curfews and cell phone use? I yearn for that kind of fight, but instead, I am a mere spectator to a fight I don't want to watch. What was once invisible has become the biggest obstacle in my life. For months I didn't even see the struggle, and for days, I didn't want to believe it. She will be all right. She is strong. She can turn things around. Maybe it is a phase. We can fix this quickly.

I underestimated her competition. I underestimated the depth of the hooks that held her in place as it relentlessly pummeled her.

She stands in the middle of the fighting ring, and I watch her waste away. We send in teams of caretakers who nurture her between rounds, fighting off the monster and tending to the numerous wounds it has already inflicted. They teach her how to fight the dragon. They arm her with tools, words, and confidence. She gathers strength, and then another round begins. It is she who must slay the dragon. It is she who must stop the monster. And I look at her, and I see her trying—but, God she is so weak. Oh, God, she is so fragile.

Please guide me, for I am lost. Please hold me, for I am helpless. I don't want to do this alone. The path is too steep, too treacherous, too risky and too unpredictable. Place my feet on the path you choose. Be my light through the darkness. Lead me and teach me. I want to learn. I want to know how to fight the evil that robs, takes and destroys. Allow me to be your hands. Put them to work or to prayer. Teach me your ways. I need you. We need you.

Of all the things you have ever given me, my daughters are the most precious gifts. Please help me help her. Please allow me to see into the crevasses of her hidden pain so that I might pour the salve of a parent's love onto them. Please, dear God, clear away from her mind the judgment she alone holds against herself and allow her to see what I see— a beautiful, tender, and courageous soul hand-crafted uniquely and most perfectly in

Praying Your Child Through Anything

the image of God. Trusting you're holding this broken mom and dad while we are holding her, Amen.

This prayer was inspired by the interview with Tom and Barbara Leopold. Tom Leopold, loving father of the suffering daughter: Tom Leopold is an American comedy writer, performer, and novelist. Among some of his most popular works are many hilarious episodes of Seinfeld and Cheers. He has also written several books and contributed speeches and jokes for presidents and other notable speakers.

Prayer Prompt

Open yourself up to the words in the St. Michael* Prayer and ask for his intercession for helping you fight against evil at home and across the world.

*Saint Michael the Archangel, defend us in battle. Be our protection against the wickedness and snares of the devil; May God rebuke him, we humbly pray; And do thou, O Prince of the Heavenly Host, by the power of God, thrust into hell Satan and all evil spirits who wander about the world seeking the ruin of souls.

Meditation Prayer for the Parents of a Child with a Life-Threatening Eating Disorder

Oh, Mighty One,

No disease has power over You. Nothing in our entire Universe has power over You, but instead bows down to Your slightest command. You, dear Lord, fashioned [name] in Your likeness and image, and You have called [him/her] to be Your heir. Almighty One, never let [name] doubt Your love for [him/her] nor that Your watchful eye absorbs [his/her] every move, thought and question.

We pray for encouragement to flow from heaven into [name] soul and for our child to hear the many prayers we utter on [his/her] behalf. Not only allow our prayers to be heard, but dear Lord, may our prayers help [name] gain energy and strength from our heartfelt message of love. Bless [him/her] with days of holy inspiration, just as You will humble [him/her] with days of weakness. Assure [name] that Your ways are true and that everything is used for Your almighty glory. Allow [him/her] to feel Your merciful love and the warmth and comfort of Your almighty arms.

We grant You our will and give You complete authority over our family. Bless us with Your peace and direction. Pour Your strength and mighty power into our home, so we together might fight the enemies who prey on our family. Amen.

The Facts: At any given time throughout the United States, it is believed eight million adolescents and young adults (mostly girls) suffer from eating disorders. The mortality rate for females 15-24 years old is twelve times higher in those suffering from anorexia than in ALL other causes of death. Most often afflicted are females between the ages of 15-35. There are three main types of eating disorders: anorexia nervosa, bulimia nervosa, and binge-eating disorder.

Praying Your Child Through Anything
...Even Depression and Self-Harm

For wisdom is mobile beyond all motion,/ and she penetrates and pervades all things by reason of purity./ And she, who is one, can do all things,/ and renews everything while herself perduring;/ and passing into holy souls from age to age/ she produces friends of God and prophets./ For she is fairer than the sun and surpasses every constellation of the stars./ Compared to light she takes precedence;/ for that, indeed, night supplants,/ but wickedness prevails not over Wisdom. Wisdom 7:24, 27, 29-30

Wisdom, a wonderous and most valuable gift from God, is not a trophy to be displayed on the mantle, and it is not gold to be secured in a safe-deposit box. Wisdom is to be used daily, like a pair of eyeglasses, for one whose sight depends on correction. For wisdom discerns wickedness and sheds light on darkness. Sometimes wisdom is inherent within a young soul (child saints and martyrs), but most often, it is earned through years of prayer, hardship, and desperate experiences.

That wisdom, the one earned, emanates from this mother and father. I could detect it instantly but later learned from the depths of where it originated. This couple's peaceful engagement with wisdom was the heavenly result gained from a series of heart-breaking experiences, near-defeat, and a painful but necessary surrender.

Wisdom has a way of pursuing us, and if we allow her to enter, she will begin guiding our actions, thoughts and words until we finally surrender ourselves completely into her care. Once surrendered, we realize her many benefits, for wickedness doesn't stand a chance against wisdom.

A Solid Start—Childhood Through Seventh Grade

Maria was one of four children, with brothers all around. Being the only girl never bothered her, and she enjoyed hanging out with her brothers and their friends. She fit right in to nearly any situation—being soft and nurturing to her youngest brother one minute and running the football with her older brother and his friends the next. She was fun to be with, confident and happy. Her life was filled with activity, good decisions, and a great work ethic inside the classroom and at home with chores. Her parents remember her as easygoing, spunky, helpful, and truthful during these early years.

The Eighth Grade Drama and Beyond

Out of the blue, as it seemed, came a new era for sweet Maria. The once-engaged child became the forever-distant one. The one sport she used to love, she now loathed. Confidence in herself was traded for a desire to fit in with the crowd. She flaunted her beauty and began discovering the doors it could open. The values and morals that used to define her were no longer even detectable. Maria sought the thrilling life, choosing manipulation as her buddy in crime. She resented the authority of her parents and developed a flippant attitude toward them.

Unprovoked, she would lash out at her family and often have cruel and piercing remarks that left everyone aghast. Almost nothing was recognizable from her childhood, as if a mean alien clone had come by night and switched places with her.

Maria's parents remember attempting calm statements and simple questions to start conversations, but Maria's lack of respect soon escalated any conversation into a dispute, ending with a demand to "straighten up" by her parents. Maria had no desire to change and thwarted their ultimatums. Unmet demands, therefore, eventually turned into yelling, grounding, removing privileges and simply wishing the whole thing a terrible nightmare they would soon wake from. They had no idea of the stronghold placed on their daughter and the master, who was now controlling the strings.

High school was particularly difficult, and her moods continued to sway as dangerous behaviors persisted. Drawing benefits from others, using her outer beauty, became an obsessive focus while her inner beauty drained like sand through an hourglass. She sought the attention of boys, and they were happy to exploit her. Her parents also noticed her choosing to spend more time at her friends' houses than her own home. With high school comes more freedom, friends who have vehicles for transportation, athletic games, extracurricular activities, and the list goes on. It provides the necessary cover for the girl who wants to isolate herself from the pack.

This negative behavior triggered a series of dark events that consumed Maria and began pulling her under as fast as it could. Conflicts arose within her as evil took hold, sending demonic nightmares to taunt and haunt her. She had taken a bite of the apple, and it became a gun to her head, happily controlling her every thought and move. Her parents would try to reach in to pull her back up, but they would be met with resistance and a severe punishment—by Maria repelling them even more and widening the chasm she had already placed between them.

When Maria was at home, she slept so she didn't have to hear her parents' whining voices saying things like, *"we don't even know you anymore, why are you doing this,* and *don't you know better than this, Maria?"* After all, this was not the way her loving parents raised her, and they certainly could not comprehend why in the world she would display such hatred toward them. They were puzzled over why she couldn't just return to her old self and once again obey her parents' rules? Those same rules had worked well for her during her twelve-plus years of life, and were still working wonders for her brothers. Strongly defending their own parenting skills and know-how, they began resisting her actions all the more. They had honestly, and with great love, built their solid reputation for raising great kids, and their daughter was single-handedly, they thought, trying to destroy it.

Never knowing when ugliness would rear its head, the family dynamics automatically shifted to support the unknown. Family fun was many times replaced with awkward silence, and many trips, outings and events were canceled or pushed back indefinitely as they feared the time bomb ticking away.

Looking at it from Maria's perspective, we can see the mounting pressure she placed on herself as she tried to understand the chemical, spiritual and emotional changes within her body. It was true that her parents were not the only ones who did not recognize

Maria. Maria didn't recognize Maria, yet she yearned for an identity and believed everyone was standing in her way of finding it. Classmates and even some friends began to turn on her as they started rumors about her, broke confidentiality, talked behind her back, excluded her from get-togethers and attacked her where they knew her to be most vulnerable. Maria's attempt to escape the pain was met with even deeper misery as she spiraled alone into the dark abyss of cutting herself, suicide attempts and panic attacks that were so terrifying, they landed her in the emergency room on a few occasions.

Rock Bottom

In the hallway of the emergency room, her mother and father nearly collapsed from the cumulative weight of years of suffering. They were in agony and they knew she was too. It became very real when Maria told them that she was willing to stop and had even tried on several occasions, but she couldn't block or rid herself of the relentless momentum built up inside her. She was now completely weakened by the force, paralyzed by its commands, and defenseless against the stronghold that now enveloped her mind and body.

Maria's mom said she felt her heart literally drop onto the floor and the breath ripped from her lungs because it hurt so deeply and crushed her to the core. It was then that her mother and father knew that controlling, helping, and understanding Maria was beyond their capabilities. If Maria, although willing, could not overturn the behavior, they knew the best chance they had at helping her would be to solicit help from others who had already traveled this treacherous road.

A once very private family called out for reinforcement. They needed a team to help them sort through the wreckage, and so they began, as always, with the one who knew Maria best, her Creator God. He helped them find the courage to completely let go and trust in His Providence. Her parents found a wilderness program that would not only help Maria but would challenge her in a positive way. The battle was on.

Praying Your Child Through Anything

The Surrender

Willingly, Maria joined her mom and dad on a twelve-hour drive to the wilderness territory, that for 40 days would be her home. It was yet another battlefield, but one hand-picked to help her overcome these powerful strongholds. She would be under strict surveillance while learning to live among teenage girls her age who were dealing with issues of their own. Perhaps this program would give her the advantage she needed and provide her new weapons to fight. Upon arrival, her mom handed her a novena prayer card* and asked her to pray it every night. Her motherly promise was to pray with her, outside, looking at the same moon and sharing the prayer that would be forever theirs.

It was a complete surrender for her mom and dad. One so intense, they would never forget the feeling. Surrender to people they did not know but trusted, to a wilderness that could be disastrous, and to the God they had never before trusted so fully and completely. It redefined their levels of faith, hope and love. In a hotel room that evening, five hours away from the daughter they left behind, her mother lay awake sobbing in the arms of her husband. As she described it, tears were all she had left to give, and so she emptied herself of even those.

Each night, bundled up in a warm blanket, her mom would open the back door of their midwestern home to a new world, one that would unite mother to daughter, instead of rip it apart. She would sit in the cold chair, oftentimes covered with snow or ice, and gaze up at the same moon lighting the path for her daughter, hoping that path would not only bring her hope but also bring her home. At one point in the novena prayer, she would insert Maria's name** and a heartfelt prayer to God about whatever was on her mind for her child. Sometimes it would be to send warmth to her in the cold temperatures, and other times, it would be for a softened heart, pure soul and joyful guidance. It was a sincere and personal prayer designed for the one daughter she factually knew to be hundreds of miles away, but that through God, the heavens and the bright moon, seemed to be cuddled right beside her.

The Family Healing Begins

The slight reprieve, from a constant defensive mode, afforded her parents the time to concentrate on the boys' activities and resume some normal family outings. Much mending and healing were required for the gashes that had been left behind in the wake of the chaos. Resuming play and enjoying each other went a long way in healing the wounds.

Surrendering her to God's care, asking for her guardian angel's protection, and calling upon the intercession of Our Blessed Mother Mary to watch over her were part of Maria's parents' daily prayers. They admitted this surrender was freeing to them, knowing that God had orchestrated the healing path. They were, once again, at peace.

Maria was allowed to write to her parents once a week and was able to receive one letter from them each week. Maria's letters were rough at first, begging to come home and resisting the surrender. They would write in their letters to Maria that they knew of her dedication and how hard she was working and that they too were working at becoming better parents for her. They were learning about her demons, hurdles and chains. They were opening their hearts and minds as to ways they could support her efforts by gaining education through online classes, learning how to help her mend what had been torn, and how to humbly and lovingly receive her back into the family. They also wrote to Maria about the lost trust and how they wanted to allow her the chance to build it once again. Healing would take time, but they were willing to give it as much time as it needed to get whole again.

The wilderness provided Maria with what they called hard and soft skills. Hard skills pertained to the physical elements of pure survival and pushing the limits. Soft skills dealt with the emotional side and concentrated heavily on coping skills and tools. She would daily have to use both to get through to the next day.

Still, it was not a magic wand that restores; therefore, patience was a requirement. Healing was slow at first, but it did come. It took time to learn, but she soon realized that it is not our loving God who kept her captive with blame, shame and distress. Through surrender, she allowed God to enter her chamber, cut the chains that bound her to evil, and offer her the gift of true freedom. Maria found her way through the wilderness and came out stronger on the other side, no longer chained but free.

The Lesson Learned and Shared for All

One thing that struck me during our talk was how Maria's mom and dad now visualize the early days of chaos and the things they would change if they had it to do over again. Maria's mom said, "We played right into the devil's playbook at the onset of her downward spiral and retreat." She explained that Maria was changing physically, spiritually, and emotionally. Once she gave in to the demons with a rash of bad decisions, they would constantly remind her of her shame and worthlessness. Her parents were validating those same feelings through frustration and disgust. The demons wanted her to see herself as a caged animal unable to spread her wings at the same time parents were cracking down on rules because of behaviors. Demons wanted her to isolate herself because, in doing so, it gave them uninterrupted access to rip at her soul.

Maria's mom reflected on those 40 days without Maria and claimed she herself was transformed. God was not only busy with Maria, but He was working on the souls of Maria's mom and dad. They grew their own faith exponentially during this time. She claimed that the divine freedom that came with divine surrender was a bit of a shock. She explained what a gift it was to relinquish everything they had and end up with more freedom, peace, and wisdom than they ever had before the family heartache. They believe a treasure like that can only be found through the heavenly handiwork, transformation and love of our Creator, God.

Maria's mom said that a parent's discipline should come from a place of love (for God is perfect love) rather than from the enmity we feel. When a child hurts on the inside, it is not easy to understand. Maria's parents believe that early and frequent communication is the key but is not easy to attain, especially with teenagers. They now know that misunderstanding her disobedience as a personal attack against them and their house rules, rather than the attack going on within herself, cost them valuable time in diagnosing the real problem.

In hindsight, they would have more calmly tried to understand from where her new struggles originated, would not have allowed themselves to be so alarmed and distressed as each new escapade reared its head, sought professional guidance more quickly, encouraged her more often when she made even slight efforts forward, and frequently they would have reminded her that she is a beloved child of God most worthy of love, mercy and forgiveness.

A Happy Ending

Maria fought the fight, front-lined the many battles and eventually won the war. Her path was strenuous, difficult, and even embarrassing at times, but she made it through. Mutual forgiveness and acceptance bound them together as a family. She and her brothers are as tight or tighter than before. They all are proud of Maria because they watched her walk the tough road and respectfully observed the many efforts she made to come back home. Maria went on to college and graduated with a degree in psychology. She has a wonderful job and recently married the love of her life.

A Prayer For Wisdom

Dear Mighty and Eternal Father,

Our daughter is struggling to survive. Darkness and evil surround her as she stares into the abyss of death. How did she get to this place and who but You can call her away from the dangerous edge she teeters on? She knows You, dear Lord God Almighty King, and has loved You since she was very young. Remind her of her many sweet prayers of intimacy with You and that her soul is marked with Your baptismal promise. She belongs to You, the Light of the World, so please shine Your power upon her soul and guide her back to You and to us. Keep her soul safe from harm as You claim Your child from the darkness. We will not rest nor cease in prayer until she is once again safely wrapped inside Your merciful arms.

As for us, her parents, please accept our total surrender. We desire the humility to lean solely on Your Providence for everything we do, say and think. As we trust that You blessed us with our daughter for such a time as this, we ask You to lead us on the righteous path You know so well. We place our full trust in the route You will choose and the guides You will hand-pick to help us along the way. We will continue, through prayer, to ask for confirmation in Your will so we can discern through Your granted wisdom the next right move, realizing her soul is under attack, and we are part of the heavenly team assigned to fight for her eternal life. Amen.

The above prayer was inspired by the interview
with Maria's mom and dad.

* **Novena** - Practiced in the Roman Catholic Church, it is a form of worship using special prayers, actions, or sacrifices for a particular intention over a period of nine successive days. The name originated from the estimated nine days of prayer offered by the apostles and disciples of Jesus between his Ascension and Pentecost. Below is the particular novena chosen by Maria's mother for their shared prayer time. St. Teresa of Calcutta, also known as Mother Teresa, is used in this particular novena as an intercessor for this request. Although the prayer honors and is directed to God alone, it is the belief that holy saints continue to pray in heaven and can intercede for the faithful as they have already been shown favor with God.

Novena Prayer to Saint Teresa of Calcutta (Mother Teresa)

Saint Teresa of Calcutta, you allowed the thirsting love of
Jesus on the Cross
to become a living flame within you,
and so became the light of His love to all.
Obtain from the Heart of Jesus...
**(insert your personal request here
for the intention you have chosen).
Teach me to allow Jesus to penetrate and possess my whole being so
completely that my life, too, may radiate His light and love to others.
Amen.

Prayer Prompt

Reflect on your child as a sweet baby, in its most humble and vulnerable place, dependent on you for everything—food, shelter, and warmth. Take this sweet image to your prayer, along with the many accomplishments they have made, the growth they have experienced, and the hardships they have endured.

Meditation Prayer for a Child Who Suffers from Depression and Self-Harm

Please help our [daughter/son]. You are the One who can reach [name] and walk [him/her] through the darkness that surrounds [him/her]. Since our words no longer penetrate [his/her] heart, please use our prayers to strengthen [him/her], that [he/she] is able to fight [his/her] way through to Your light, Your goodness, and Your mercy.

Our hearts break when we watch our child suffer, and we feel so inadequate and helpless against the enemies that overshadow [him/her]. We will empty ourselves of all our fears, disappointments and frustrations, but humbly ask You to fill the emptiness with wisdom, understanding and patience. We have turned [his/her] care over to You and are but instruments in Your hand. If Your will is for [him/her] to get help, please guide us to the safe places You trust and to the people who will speak and demonstrate Your Almighty truth.

Help our family, dear Lord, be forever attentive to our eternal mission. Our crosses are heavy, but Your love sweetens the road we must travel, and we feel Your strength working through us. Only through You can we dare to plunge to such depths, and only through You can we dare to rise to such heights. Only through You can we reach this suffering soul. Amen.

Praying Your Child Through Anything
...Even When Your Rebellious Teen
Challenges Your Patience

But the wisdom from above is first of all pure, then peaceable, gentle, compliant, full of mercy and good fruits, without inconstancy or insincerity. And the fruit of righteousness is sown in peace for those who cultivate peace. James 3: 17-18

In 2014, my husband and I visited our dear friends, Jeff and Karen Saturday, who, nine months earlier, had moved from Indiana to the Atlanta area. Georgia was where Jeff and Karen were raised and was still home for many of their family. In 1999, Jeff and Karen moved to Indianapolis for the next step in Jeff's NFL career, and it became their "home away from home" where many strong roots were planted in their new community. Some of their greatest memories were created in Indianapolis, starting with the births of their three children, Jeffrey, Savannah, and Joshua. At the time they moved, Joshua was eight years old, Savannah was twelve, and Jeffrey was fourteen. The children had loved visiting their grandmas, grandpas, aunts, uncles and cousins in the Atlanta area, but their heart, home and friends were all in Indiana. It was the only home they had ever known.

With a career change for Jeff that no longer required an Indiana residence, Jeff and Karen began feeling a strong tug at their hearts to move the family south, back to the place they were raised and where many family members still lived. Once the decision to move was made, they broke the news to the children.

The Challenge

The younger two children took the news rather well; they were indeed sad but also excited for the change. Jeffrey was angry. In fact, he was insistent that they were making a huge mistake and informed his parents that he would NOT be moving with them. His friends reinforced his judgment and advised him to stand firm against this insane idea to uproot their home and family. Further, Jeffrey was told he was welcome to move in with one of his close friends and visit his parents in Georgia during summer break and the holidays! It tore at Jeff and Karen's hearts that their eldest son resisted all reason and was unwilling to even discuss the move. Possibly most hurtful was that he accused them of making the decision flippantly, with selfish motives, and without prayer. Little did Jeffrey know that it was in prayer that the stirring to move came, but it was also through prayer Jeff and Karen asked for direction, and it was because of prayer they had finally acquired the peace needed to move forward with the decision.

Still, Jeffrey's resistance intensified and cut deeply, causing unwanted strife, insecurity, tension, and resentment within the household. In his eyes, Indiana was their home… and had been all of his life. Jeffrey experienced a painful move the year before, when during his first semester of his eighth grade school year, the family was uprooted for his father's one-year contract with the Green Bay Packers. Jeffrey learned quickly that he didn't like leaving his Indiana friends and having to adjust to a new school. The Green Bay move was difficult, but life was finally calm again upon their return to Indianapolis, as everyone settled back into the familiar routines of school and friends. Jeffrey was overjoyed to be home when, what seemed to be totally out of the blue, he got the news they were about to move again. This time, however, they weren't coming back. Jeffrey was not going to give up fighting until his parents saw the foolishness of their absolutely absurd plan.

Throughout these battles, Jeff and Karen wondered if this move was worth all of the mayhem it was causing or if they should contemplate bringing peace back by postponing or canceling the move. It was heartbreaking…and terribly frustrating for them. But God was always there, confirming through friends or family that the course they were on was the one they were to follow.

Heavenly Arbitration

Pleading for Almighty assistance to help sort through the family wreckage, God placed on Jeff and Karen's hearts to bring their son into their prayers—not just in word or thought but to physically place Jeffrey beside them as they prayed together. Cooperating with the inspiration of the Holy Spirit, Jeff and Karen gave it a try.

Awkward at first, the three of them poured out their requests to God, the Almighty arbitrator. Jeff and Karen asked God to please place, on all of their hearts, the best decision for the family as a whole. They called out to God about Jeffrey's hurtful resistance toward them and how much his disobedience disappointed them. But they also requested God to soften their hearts to understand where Jeffrey's challenges and insecurities were rooted.

First, God helped open the heart of Jeff and Karen to remember Jeffrey's distinctive nature, moral fiber and honorable qualities as a human being; the very characteristics that had given his mom and dad the confidence they needed to support their decision to move, believing Jeffrey could thrive in his new environment. They were so proud of everything Jeffrey had accomplished, and they knew, because of his determination and work ethic, he would be able to recreate meaningful relationships in a new school. Jeff and Karen explained to Jeffrey how valuable it would be for all of their children to be surrounded by faith-filled grandparents and extended family. Jeffrey had not considered the impact of extended family because he believed his family was what he had built in Indiana. He was fine having the "out-of-towners" visit occasionally but didn't see why a move to be near them was so important.

Next, God showed Jeff and Karen Jeffrey's vulnerabilities, which helped them understand his apprehension to leave. Jeffrey's personality was unreserved. Whatever he did, he did with great passion and unwavering commitment. This made the thought of uprooting even more painful. He was invested... "all in," so to speak. He didn't just have friends; they were his confidants. He was not just a spectator of life, but rather an active participant. It wasn't just being part of a team that energized Jeffrey, it was his role as leader that gave him a greater sense of self-worth. Jeffrey made school his life's work and had built lasting relationships with the students, teachers, and administration. It was agonizing and scary for him to process the work ahead of him, knowing how long it had taken him to find the faithful friends he now felt honored to be around. Jeffrey wondered how he could ever fit into a new school that, most likely, had already established their cliques and social groups. He worried that he would forever be the odd man out. He was very familiar with that "new kid" feeling from his months in Green Bay and couldn't imagine having to walk that tightrope again, especially without the safety net of knowing it was short-lived and he could return to the comforts of home in Indiana. Everything Jeffrey had worked so hard to attain and maintain was being ripped from him as if his parents didn't care.

God revealed to them, through praying together, that Jeffrey's heart was broken, and his life seemed shattered. Jeffrey needed his parents to understand him as much as Jeff and Karen needed him to understand them. Jeff and Karen could have pulled the parent "trump" card out at any time, totally exhausted from the banter, but that is not how God persuades us. Just as God demonstrated, rather than dictated, His love for us through a suffering Son, He asked Jeff and Karen to lead, love, and guide Jeffrey through his pain. With prayer and patience, they began to earn Jeffrey's trust and God transformed their family. Although Jeffrey still didn't want to move, he honored his prayerful parents with his loving obedience, trusting them with his new life that was about to unfold.

What became of this struggling family? Find the inspirational answers in their prayer, captured nine months after they moved south, and then even more insight in the update interview, six years later.

A Prayer for Heavenly Arbitration

Dear God,

Thank You for being the only friend to jump in the car with us to move across the country! We needed Your calming spirit sitting right beside us. It was difficult for our family to leave the many good friends and homey comforts behind, knowing that our new life was filled with a host of unfamiliar people, places, and things. Every day was filled with new challenges and opportunities. It took time to transform an empty house into our home, our space, and our future. We drove around learning the lay of the land, the shortcuts, and the traffic patterns. Everything was new; exciting and overwhelming at the same time. When things got stressful and doubt began to set in, You kept squarely on our hearts that we had followed Your lead and that we were in Your care.

As You know, Jeffrey especially had a difficult time with this move. We saw the hurt he was experiencing and the painful struggles it caused him. We watched him closely those first few months, praying he would someday soon feel at home in this new place. We asked you to soften his heart to his new surroundings and to open his eyes to the friendships You planned for him. You are the family mediator, and we trust You completely, knowing all will happen in Your divine timing and for Your glory. We see You at work in his life and we celebrate every breakthrough, no matter how insignificant it may seem.

Thank you for trusting us with the cross of this move and for supplying us with the strength we needed to leave our wonderful friendships behind. In Your goodness, You allowed the extensive miles separating us from our Indiana friends to shrink as we still feel the strength of their love and support from afar. Thank You for the extended family that embraced our decision, the encouragement they give us daily, and for the opportunity our children now have to hear grandparents cheering them on at every event. Sometimes we try to imagine life without them nearby, and we cannot. We are blessed that with every new day, You show us more ways to love and cherish our new surroundings. Through your precious Son, Jesus, we pray, Amen.

This prayer was inspired by the interview with Jeff and Karen Saturday. Jeff is a former NFL Indianapolis Colts center, Super Bowl champion and currently a sports analyst for ESPN television. The deep faith of both Jeff and Karen are exemplary.

A Six-year Update on the Saturday Family

From Jeff Saturday's perspective:

The father, Jeff Saturday, reflects on the move and believes even more today in the Divine Providence that brought this family back to their Georgia roots. Jeff said that he had wanted to give his children the gift of having extended family close by, a benefit he was not afforded in his youth. He knew the treasure chest that awaited them was filled with love, wisdom, and intimate family moments, but he could not have imagined the constant joy it would bring.

It is the influence they impart on each other through spending time together that brings a smile to his face. He often hears his three children echoing their grandparents' words without even knowing it. However, Jeff knows exactly which of the four grandparents planted that particular seed. He believes that when you are blessed enough to have Godly parents, why wouldn't you do everything you can to bring them closer to the lives of your children? The extended family dynamics provide much needed parental reinforcement and fortifies his and Karen's faith as much as it does the children's.

Jeff explained that being present is where life really matters. Relationships, he believes, have to be slow-cooked, fostered, and nurtured. This one-on-one time between grandparents and grandchildren has reaped many tangible rewards and, undoubtedly, some yet to be discovered. The value of the wisdom they bestow on inquisitive minds is priceless. Even if parents and grandparents differ on issues, it allows children the gifts of perspective and discernment.

As we were talking on the phone, Jeff began to chuckle. Two great examples of what he was just trying to explain surfaced at that very moment. His mom had just texted him an article, The Influence of Godly Parents, while his daughter sat only a few yards away talking on her cell phone to her grandfather. Once again, the two were collaborating on another tough homework assignment in a subject, Jeff claims, they equally should have earned a grade. Yes, God knew to what blessings He was calling this family. They had a choice, and it was not an easy one to make, but they found their way home through trust and obedience.

From Jeffrey Saturday's perspective:

Jeffrey admitted that he was a real pain in everyone's side the first eight or nine months following the move to Georgia. He made it his job to point out every challenge they faced and wouldn't let a single setback be forgotten. His secret scheme was to make it so miserable that they would consider moving back home to Indiana since, as he saw it, things were not going as his parents had planned. Jeffrey even refused to invest in new friendships, certain that he would soon be back at school with his old buddies. Every evening, after school, Jeffrey would spend hours on the phone, or playing online games with his "real" friends from Indiana, avoiding the temporary ones in Georgia.

Once Jeffrey realized his family was in Georgia to stay, he said he began letting his guard down and allowing grandparents and extended family in. He also changed the way he acted at school and began to make new friends. Slowly Jeffrey opened his heart to a new way of life and embraced the opportunity he was given.

Early life in Georgia turned out to be quite a roller coaster for Jeffrey with a few highs and some plummeting lows. After getting comfortable in one school for the first year, his parents thought it might be better to switch schools again, this time to offer each child a school with fewer students and smaller class sizes. He can now claim, with a chuckle, that he truly believed his parents did that "because they wanted me in the most pain I could possibly be in!" Increasing Jeffrey's angst, after the change of schools, he experienced a series of athletic setbacks with a serious concussion and later, a fractured spine. Jeffrey's faith waivered greatly during these trials, and he admits he was mad at himself, but even more so... he was mad at God.

With the clear vision time provides, Jeffrey can now see that through all of the heartache and heavy crosses came many blessings, in fact, too many to count. His close friends, from both Georgia and Indiana, didn't give up on him when he was laid up for an entire summer as his spine slowly and painfully healed. If he couldn't participate in the summer outside activities like swimming and playing ball, his friends insisted they visit him at home, spending hours playing games, watching movies, or just talking. Jeffrey also spoke of the unselfish teachers who personally took their free time to coach him through every assignment. He had humble and endearing therapists that he claims were nothing short of angels.

They showed him undeserved kindness when he was hurting so badly and would even make a house call between visits to check on his progress. And, of course, there was his wonderful family, including the many extended ones who loved on him like never before. Every soul he encountered was a gift from God, and he knew it. They possessed God's mercy, and they lived His kindness. Jeffery believes he learned more in his prolonged downtime than he ever would have from his many activities.

When the time came for Jeffrey to reenter the football field his senior year, he said it was like a slice of heaven. It was as if God Himself, or possibly a heaven-sent bodyguard, were there with him, because he continuously felt a divine presence surrounding him. Every time he ran a great play or scored a touchdown, he pointed up to the Man responsible. His joy was so palpable that the spectators and teammates wanted a part of it. He knew exactly where this feeling was coming from, and he never wanted it to end. In fact, Jeffrey was totally content staying right where he was, soaking in the glory and conceding the patience it cost him to get there.

The college application process proved to be another challenge. He had procrastinated as long as he possibly could because he couldn't imagine another move, especially one where his family would not follow. He shuttered at the thought of missing all of his sister's and brother's sporting events and activities. He had loved being a part of the Saturday family clan that always gathered to cheer at every game. Wanting to play college football, but having missed his junior year of high school when players are often recruited, he was left with an uncertain football future. No matter what college option he entertained, it always ended in heartache, as he anticipated leaving behind everyone that he had come to treasure.

When the dust finally settled and the deadlines closed in, Jeffrey made a decision. He was headed to play football for the University of North Carolina Tar Heels. Players had to report in the early summer, so Jeffrey had to leave home while graduation parties and summer relaxation were in full swing. He said about that first year away, "not being around my family every day was so hard. Most kids were happy to get away, but it was really tough for me, and I missed everyone so very much."

Jeffrey shared with me a valuable lesson he learned as a young man that many of us adults still struggle with. He said, "God has confirmed for me... He doesn't like it when I am comfortable." Every time it happens, God stretches him to do something else, and many times, it is a painful journey way outside the comfort zone he establishes for himself. He said it took him long enough to see it, but he is learning to play the game God created for him... and it is almost always... a bit uncomfortable!

Prayer Prompt

Sometimes we just want to answer a child's why with, "because I said so, that's why." And there are times when that may be an appropriate response, but in other situations, God will provide us with another opportunity to deliver a more profound and lasting message. Conflict can arise as an opportunity to help us learn and grow from each other. We can forget that what God places as peace on our heart may remain unsettled for someone else within the family. Do you ever wonder if God does that on purpose, so that we need to work and pray together to do His will? Ask God to reveal the places that need attention, prayer, and better communication.

Praying Your Child Through Anything

Meditation Prayer For a Rebellious Child Who Challenges Your Patience

Dear Lord,
Please open my heart to Your prompting and help me be an example to [name]. Give me the courage to physically invite [him/her] into the sacred space I normally reserve for just You and me so [he/she] may better understand my most intimate prayers for this family. If our hearts remain closed to each other's expectations, please send us a measure of sweet perseverance, necessary to overcome our bitterness and fortify our waning patience. Fill our souls with the powerful *Seven Gifts of the Holy Spirit.**

We adore and revere You, O Lord God and seek Your guidance.
Allow us to see as You see, with *wisdom, knowledge* and *understanding*.
Open our eyes to the wolves who feed on anger and resentment; they are eager to devour our family's love.
Gather Your fearful servants from the separate corners of the boxing ring into Your loving arms; never let us leave Your secure embrace.
Please mediate our cause and judge our requests with Your almighty and *wise counsel*.
Pour out upon us the *fortitude* to accept Your prescription for healing and Your judgment over our misunderstandings. We know Your love will never steer us wrong but will bring peace to our home.

Help us to see each other with Your most tender eyes of true and forgiving love. Knit us together, heart to heart and mind to mind, so we may walk in unison as we follow Your plan for our family. Amen.

*The gifts of the Holy Spirit, taken from Isaiah 11: 2-3, are: wisdom, understanding, counsel, fortitude, knowledge, piety, and fear of the Lord.

Praying Your Child Through Anything
...Even When Your Child Chooses to Struggle Alone

"The soul whom God wants to draw to deepest union with him by means of holy prayer, must pass through the way of suffering during prayer." St. Paul of the Cross

I have known and admired this woman for years. She is perfect, in my mind. She is beautiful, soft-spoken, caring, endearing, and engaging. When she speaks to you, you are the only one in the world to her. As one might imagine from such a person, she has dedicated much of her life to helping others.

From my vantage point, I not only thought she was perfect, but that her life was as well. She was the mom who rose extra early every morning to make homemade muffins and a healthy breakfast for her family before they would part for their day of school or work. She has always been loyal to her family, to her friends, and to her work. Most of all, she is loyal to her faith in God. That is where the inner-peace I so admire in her comes from.

I met my perfect friend with the perfect life for lunch and was telling her about my book and asked her if she might know of any families that might be interested in sharing a story of faith with me. She had the perfect person in mind.

It was her own story she would share with me, so others could find hope through her long and difficult journey. She seemed to be trying to convince me she was not the perfect person I once thought. Her many bouts with darkness over recent years did not alter my perception; in fact, the depths of her struggles revealed even a stronger woman than I had imagined. She is perfect through Christ Jesus, and His light reflects even brighter through her, as I learned her story of faith, perseverance, and prayer.

A Child Struggles, A Mom Reflects

A mother's heart detects cracks in the foundation of a child's heart before they can be seen or heard. She searched for the moment and time that her son's behavior first showed signs of distress and prayed for a clue that would provide the cause. She hoped that if she could find the source of trouble, she could help fix the problem. But what she found went so much deeper than a simple question and a simple answer. Her adult son was now living away from home, so she was only able to catch glimpses of what she perceived as desolation. She knew by the words spoken and even the ones left unspoken that there was enormous pain, anxiety, and suffering going on within his soul.

Reflecting back, she remembered times when the middle-school bullies preyed on him in his youth and how his once-soft heart hardened in defense. No matter how obscure and faulty the accusations lobbed at him from his peers seemed to be, it pecked away at who he was, what he believed, and how he thought. During this time, she saw him retreat and try to isolate himself but, fortunately, she was right there beside him to speak truth and guide him through the rough patches. Mom and son talked through the pains and, for a time, everything seemed to be under control.

The son went to college and left behind the numerous comforts that came from living at home. College can be a time of great growth and change, but for her son, it became a slippery slope of giving in to temptation. His self-esteem and confidence plummeted, and she saw flashes of bitter anger and resentment. She was wondering, because of his curt and cruel manner toward seemingly everyone, if he now had become the bully. Excessive amounts of liquor became his coping mechanism, and she worried about his safety.

A Different Way to Reach Him

When her son was falling into the darkness of the world, it was God she chose to tether herself to. It was from the pleading depths of her prayers that she was able to vividly discern the God-given gifts He was sending to her. The days of consoling her son in her arms or speaking wisdom to his heart were gone. Mom's gentle kiss and smile could no longer soothe his fears. Her words of truth and concern were falling on deaf ears. As instructed by God, she dropped the backpack full of the usual mom tools and began a more weightless climb behind Jesus, trusting he had a better way to reach her son's brokenness.

She dug in deeper to her prayer life, filling herself up with God's love and peaceful thoughts. Each day for more than eight years, she worked through a specific routine to strengthen herself and give glory and honor to God. Part of her disciplined practice was to seek answers through both contemporary books and ancient writings of Holy Scripture and the lives of the saints. She also recited a daily novena* of prayer and contemplation to our Heavenly Mother Mary as well as journaling her thoughts on both despair and thanksgiving. Her consistent prayers, journal entries, and novenas were specifically tailored to abolish the strongholds that had taken residence within her son.

Hope

Ever so slowly, she began to see sprinklings of hope. Perhaps the seeds of faith that were planted so many years ago found fertile ground, food, and a ray of sunlight. Her son began talking about a deacon who was inspiring him to see things in a different light. It was sound and sage advice that loosened the chains, but it did not break him free. It was a struggle for her son, but God would continue to send in much-needed reinforcements— and some of those would be strong enough to penetrate his soul and break down the walls of isolation. New friends and a sweet lady would enter her son's life, and he would cautiously allow them into his world. As if trust and confidence were rungs on a ladder leading him from depression to the light, her son would patiently climb them each day to a new and brighter world.

She was certain the journaling aided her in humility and gave her perspective. Without this tool of divine measurement, she might easily have overlooked the vast contrast between where this perilous journey with her son began and how far God's love and grace had taken her.

She will forever cherish a call from her son in the midst of numerous prayers. He just called to chat, which had not happened for years. As they spoke, he asked her a truly sincere and heartfelt question. "How are *you* doing, mom?" She thought to herself, how in the world would she possibly begin to answer that question? With the prompting of the Holy Spirit, she found the words and said, "I'm so proud of you, son. And when you are okay, I am okay."

A Prayer for Guidance to Reach Him Through the Maze

Dear Gracious Lord,

Is this suffering young man the same son who always sought my companionship and advice? Is this the son whose sweet and humble smile could turn any bad day to pure joy? When did his steps begin to turn from me? Did he slowly walk, run, or fly away from the ones who love him? I looked around, and he was so far away that I hardly recognized him. He looks different, yet somehow the same, as if he is hidden behind a mask that distorts his charm and complicates his being.

I pray in earnest to You for him. I trust that in time You will reach him, and I ask You to soften his heart, hardened over time by the cruelty and temptations of this world. He stands at a confusing intersection where his doubts, shame, and guilt point him toward a road of more heartache, pain, and struggle. Anger and resentment are his weapons for coping, and the cycle repeats itself time and again.

I know You can change people because You have changed me. Once a private person of prayer, I neither wished to share my trials nor wanted to bother anyone with a request for prayer for my family. I now find myself opening doors to others, so their beautiful prayers might unite with mine and support me. I have found the experience of others brings me much-needed comfort and peace. I no longer worry about the judgment by others but seek the wisdom of Your work within them. I would never have known of Your mighty graces flourishing throughout this community if You had not encouraged me to open my doorway of pain to find them.

Praying Your Child Through Anything

How could I have ever anticipated this path? It has been rugged, frustrating, and even completely dark at times. Tears have soaked my eyes, and I have often fallen to my knees in complete surrender. I begged You to afford me a glimmer of light as I felt my trust and faith in my own son weaken. Your loving manner has redirected and simplified my hopes and dreams for him, and You have taught me not only to trust in You but also in the son I love. You remind me often of the good seeds planted within him and that he belongs to You. You have claimed him, and You have already forgiven him. You shine light on the simplest things he does, and You share Your encouragement with me. If not through Your eyes, I would not see the hope You see. Sometimes I feel so close to You on this path, that I hope I don't stumble on Your sandals! Amen.

This prayer was inspired by the interview with an anonymous mom.

* **Novena-** Practiced in the Roman Catholic Church, it is a form of worship using special prayers, actions, or sacrifices for a particular intention over a period of nine successive days. The mother in this story continued this practice for over eight consecutive years. The name, Novena, originated from the estimated nine days of prayer offered by the apostles and disciples of Jesus between his Ascension and Pentecost. St. Monica, instrumental in the 17-year-long conversion of her son St. Augustine, is used as an intercessor in this particular novena. Although the prayer honors and is directed to God alone, it is the belief that holy saints continue to pray in heaven and can intercede for the faithful as they have already been shown favor with God.

Novena Prayer for Parents

St. Monica is a powerful intercessor because of her example of faith and endurance in praying for the conversion of her son, St. Augustine. Day 1 through 9, recite the prayer below. You are encouraged to recite this prayer daily and pray for the intentions of all those who are also reciting this prayer:

Eternal and merciful Father, I give You thanks for the gift of Your Divine Son who suffered, died, and rose for all mankind. I thank You also for my Catholic faith and ask Your help that I may grow in fidelity by prayer, by works of charity and penance, by reflection on Your Word, and by regular participation in the Sacraments of Penance and the Holy Eucharist.

You gave Saint Monica a spirit of selfless love manifested in her constant prayer for the conversion of her son Augustine. Inspired by boundless confidence in Your power to move hearts and by the success of her prayer, I ask the grace to imitate her constancy in my prayer for [name] who no longer shares in the intimate life of your Catholic family. Grant through my prayer and witness that (he/she) may be open to the promptings of Your Holy Spirit and return to loving union with Your Church. Grant also that my prayer be ever hopeful and that I may never judge another, for You alone can read hearts. I ask this through Christ, our Lord. Amen.

Saint Monica, pray for us!

Prayer Prompt

Reflect on how you interact with your family and ask God to show you divine avenues to their souls that perhaps you did not know existed.

Meditation Prayer for a Parent Whose Child Chooses to Struggle Alone

Oh, my sweet love and Almighty God,

My child is struggling alone, and my heart is throbbing. I beg You, dear Lord, to help me find a way to reach [name]. I fear [he/she] only hears bitterness or worry when I speak, even when I am careful, for the enemy spins my words into confusion. Open my ears to hear Your whispers of hope for my [son/daughter]. Calm my heart with Your patient and steady rhythm of blessings and mercy. I send You to [him/her], my almighty and eternal advocate, for only Your powers can seep through locked doors and into closed minds. You must go and keep watch over the one I love.

Please give [name] the ears to hear Your voice above the chaos of the world. Help [him/her] feel the energy behind the gifts and friendships You send daily to help [him/her] jump each hurdle and carry each cross. Allow [name] to trust in Your promises of eternity and help [him/her] distinguish between Your heavenly blessings and the empty pleasures of the world. I pray for Your light to penetrate and heal the brokenness of [his/her] soul. Lead [name] back to You.

You alone know from where the pain originated and how deep and wide it runs. I place my child and my heartfelt prayers into Your powerful hands. Amen.

Praying Your Child Through Anything
...Even When He Announces His Same-Sex Attraction

"The greatest grace God can give someone is to send him a trial he cannot bear with his own powers—and then sustain him with his grace so he may endure to the end and be saved." Saint Justin Martyr

I met his mother for lunch to hear her story. I heard about her through a friend and knew that this woman was a heavy-duty prayer warrior. We began the conversation with a look at her life as a mother of three. Two of her three pregnancies occurred close together, having her first two sons in a quick three-year time frame. Hoping for more children, she was disappointed when another baby did not follow immediately. She always felt in her heart that she would have three children, so she waited it out. Several times she suspected she might be pregnant, but each time, her suspicion was proven wrong. She remembered asking God, "I just feel I'm supposed to have three children, so if that is the case, why, God, are you holding this third baby back from me?"

She even found herself praying for this third child— that she was confident God knew and loved from the beginning of time but was yet to be given to her. She prayed for a kind and sweet-tempered child. The world could use more of those, she thought. She also prayed the child would be "spirited" and bring joy into their home and into this world. She said, looking back, it was odd to think of how she so fervently prayed for this child, never really knowing if God would choose to bless her with another baby. Still, she prayed and waited.

She remembers a time when she finally gave up, resigned to the fact that she missed her opportunity to be blessed with a third child. During this waiting period, she immersed herself in a series of Bible studies, inspirational speakers, and sacred readings that she dearly cherished. She found herself being filled with wisdom and good people at every turn. Life was good!

At the age of thirty-seven and seven years after the birth of her youngest child, the pregnancy test read positive. Indeed, God had sent the third child she longed for. From the moment she knew she was pregnant, she felt she knew this baby and was convinced that all her solemn prayers were soon to be answered. This child was destined to be kind, sweet-tempered, and spirited. She couldn't wait to meet him!

The baby arrived, and he was the answer to each of her specific prayers and more. Everyone loved him, and he brought abundant joy to every place he went and to every person he came in contact with. He was an old soul, true to friendships, happy, kind, and genuine. His teachers could always depend on him to do whatever task was needed, and he was their joy within the classroom.

Unfortunately, all of that began to change when the kids at school began to point out his "flaws." His kind-heartedness seemed totally out of place in a middle school fueled by competition, judgment, and insecurity. He found himself on the outside looking in, abandoned, and all alone. Students, one by one, fell in line with the leaders to chastise his every action or simply alienate him. In school, there was a risk to a classmate who was caught talking to him, and even a high price was set if you even contemplated being his friend. Guarded by teachers and loved by the administration, he was peacefully guided through each day, taking tests in another room, even though he didn't academically require help or extra time.

She loved him all the more as he walked the lonely stretch through middle and then high school. He dated some and had a few friends, but he never truly seemed to find his place. Thoughts began to enter her mind that perhaps her child might walk a different path.

On a return visit from college, at twenty years of age, her son came home with news he could hardly wait to share. His joy could not be contained as he spoke of finding an incredible love and the happiness he had always longed for. Not even concerned that she might take pause, he told her that his love was a man, nine years his senior, and that he had met him on the internet. The rest of the day was a blur as she wrestled with thoughts and fears. One obvious fear was that her son was being used and manipulated by an older person he had met on the internet, a fear any parent would have. And, not to mention the realization that her son had just told her he was gay.

The surprise revelation left her with a flood of emotions. At the time, she was crushed, disappointed, and worried for her son. She looked at this cross her son would carry and wondered how this new information would change the trajectory of their family's lives.

With all these emotions swirling around in her head, she knew she needed the comfort and wisdom of God and soon took all of her worries, concerns, and fears to diligent and thoughtful prayer. Immediately, peace returned to her soul with the distinct calmness she had experienced while waiting for this third child. She was filled with wisdom, understanding, and countless graces. God had also surrounded her with holy people, and she had a loving and devoted husband who would strengthen her while together they traversed this new and unknown territory.

Although her son's first homosexual relationship soon ended, her son was consistent with his newfound sexuality, and she worried about his open promiscuity. How was she to live with such a contradiction between her beloved faith and her beloved son? She still trusted that marriage was created solely for one man and one woman and held tightly to the Catholic Church's teaching on homosexuality. So, how was she supposed to handle this paradox brewing within her home?

God did not ask her to bend her faith in any way. In fact, her peace was there because she held tightly to the truth. She quickly learned that love trumps all when it comes to the children God places into our care and that only God has access to the divine measuring tool He will use to judge our souls in the end. Earthly measuring sticks are not worthy of nor are capable of judging someone's love. She realized her role was to pray fervently for her child, encourage him to keep his faith in God strong, and hand him over to the Mighty One who perfects hearts and judges souls with fatherly attention, grace, and mercy.

Another mother's words came rushing into her mind as she contemplated her next move with her son. Before any of this happened, she once asked a dear friend in a similar situation what she did when she found out her daughter was a lesbian. Her courageous friend smiled at her and said, "You just love them, of course."

And that is what she did. Love sometimes means to defend, and sometimes it means to question. Sometimes love requires us to shield our loved ones, and sometimes it requires us to prepare them. Sometimes love means to giggle and be present while simply enjoying the person God created them to be. Sometimes it means we fall to our knees, begging for the graces to love them the way God does and to be His voice, His hugs, and His encouragement. Always, not just sometimes, love is found when we allow God to show us the way.

Teach Us the Ways of Your Love

Dear Father God,

We come before You, humbled that You blessed our family with three children whom we love and cherish. Each child is unique and blesses us with different opportunities to both teach and to grow. We know that our love for our children is only surpassed by Your Divine love for them and, therefore, we ask You to guide us throughout this tender journey.

We know Your will is rooted in love. Our son seeks to love and be loved, like no one I have ever known. Help him find love in this world; the love You have chosen for him. Let it be designed by You, perfected by You, sent by You, and ordained by You. For what he seeks, let there be an answer, and for the crosses he must bear, let him have the strength to endure.

We beg You, dear Lord God, to instill in him the desire to follow Your divine will. Help us encourage and support this child You created for the purpose You desire. Sow wisdom back into our culture, where blurry fields of sexuality are commonplace, and help us rediscover the genius of Your Almighty plan for all peoples. Through Your precious Son's name, we ask all these things. Amen.

This prayer was inspired by the interview with a loving mom.

Prayer Prompt

When our faith is challenged or feels uncomfortable, seek His Truth. He will give us the grace to overcome the temptations of the world. Lean on Him for every truth you are seeking.

Meditation Prayer for a Child With Same-Sex Attraction

Dear God,

I consecrate* [name] to You. [He/She] is searching for something, and I know that something is You. Shepherd their heart toward Your Son, the Good Shepherd, who will keep them safe in a confusing world. You, dear Omnipotent one, have ordered our lives in such a way to overlay peace and joy atop the sorrows and crosses we must bear.

A heavenly lens reveals the light of Your love in all circumstances. You have created us for love, and in loving others, we are doing Your will. The world taints heavenly perspectives, and it calls Your way rigid and outdated. Please guide each of us, Your humble and naïve little ones, to the truth in Your ways, where freedom to love one another is provided to all.

Help [name] see as You see and to love as You love, for through that heavenly and eternal adoration, [he/she] will enjoy everlasting life. Instruct us to be good examples for our children like You are to us. Magnify Your holy way within our hearts as You blot out the ways of the world. Purify our hearts so we can see clearly Your intentions and understand Your infinite and perfect love. Amen.

*Consecration of Yourself and Children – A Roman Catholic tradition used to declare something or someone for the Sacredness of God. Many countries, states, and churches have been consecrated to God for His will and holy works. Likewise, a person may also consecrate themselves or their loved ones to God. There are many books written to aid us in the consecration process, and most use 33 days of consistent prayer in exchange for this special and holy protection. The 33 days are believed to be long enough to help us establish a healthy habit and a solid pattern of desire. It also equates to one day for each year Jesus Christ lived on Earth before His crucifixion.

Praying Your Child Through Anything
...Even the Sudden Death of a Beloved Father

In the same way, the Spirit too comes to the aid of our weakness; for we do not know how to pray as we ought, but the Spirit itself intercedes with inexpressible groanings. And the one who searches hearts knows what is the intention of the Spirit, because it intercedes for the holy ones according to God's will. Romans 8:26-27

Nancy's story became my first interview for this book. God had inspired my desire to write the stories that fall on these pages, but I didn't fully understand the impact they might have until I met Nancy. She, like many after her, told their story with their eyes. A parent's pain runs deep, and their eyes will many times disclose secret passages to their heart.

Nancy is a warm and sweet-tempered lady. She is inviting and inclusive to all, yet there is a shy side to her too. She laughs softly and smiles often. She is a good soul, for sure!

We were on pilgrimage in New York City, and Nancy was a part of our small group. The first night was spent getting to know each other. As we went around the room, we each told a little bit about ourselves and where we were from. Nancy finished telling us about herself, and the priest leading our group asked her if he could share more about her story and why she was in New York City. She nodded yes, and he respectively gave witness to a story I will never forget.

Our pilgrimage took place in December of 2015, and to be exact, it had been over fourteen years since Nancy had taken the train ride into the heart of the city. New York City held deep and special meaning to her, and she didn't want to spend this reunion with just anyone, so she booked the trip, which was to be led by Fr. Leo Patalinghug. Nancy knew this would be a difficult journey as she traversed the city that held, for her, both warm and gut-wrenching memories.

The Day to Remember

Looking back, that sunny day in September was a morning that began like most others. Dennis, her husband, left their home for a day at work. He traveled into the city where he entered the North Tower, pushed the elevator floor marked 101, and met his fellow workers just as he had done so many times before. This day was to be different. It was September 11, 2001— a day marked in history forever!

Like many with loved ones who worked in or around the World Trade Center, Nancy nervously paced in anticipation for the phone to ring or the door to burst open. She yearned to hear his voice and the words describing an unforeseen delay that kept him from work that day. Her mind held onto the hope that maybe he had an errand to run in the morning that had kept him far away from the Twin Towers. She waited, but he never phoned. She watched, but he never burst through the front door. He was gone, and a dull numbness filled her entire body. The overwhelming sadness of the unexpected reality cut her to the core.

Nancy spent days retreating into her bed or slouched on the couch. Standing took energy and, frankly, she was empty. With two small children, whose needs and questions she could hardly manage, Nancy found herself longing for the safety, warmth, and comfort of her bed, pondering a very uncertain future without Dennis.

Reeling through her mind were thoughts and images of Dennis. She was tortured by the fate of her beloved. Did he suffer? Was he able to spend his last moments comforting those around him like he had always done for his own family? Nancy's heart could not even imagine what Dennis experienced. The nightmares did not discriminate and filled both days and nights, awake or asleep, calm or tense.

Cantor Fitzgerald Financial Services Company occupied the 101st through the 105th floors with 960 employees. Dennis was one of 658 coworkers who died when the hijacked airliner flew into the 93rd through the 99th floors of the World Trade Center. Every soul, 658 persons, who reported to work that morning before 8:48 A.M.

perished in the attack. Nancy knew many of them by name and the families they left behind. Her heart yearned to reach out, but she didn't know exactly where to begin because she was barely surviving herself.

Nancy's children, who needed her in ways she felt ill-equipped to handle, had their own unique path of navigating the loss of their father. Normally within a community, sorrow is found in droplets here and there, while each person does what they can to support the few in need. This suffering was different. It was a tsunami of sorrow and extended further than her neighborhood, city, or state. This piercing pain affected an entire nation, and Nancy was at the epicenter.

Nancy found that even when an entire nation is mourning, it still gives rise to generous and caring souls. They will find the courage to tend to the weak, the lost, and the heartbroken. Food was the healing method of choice, and it was supplied in abundance. Daily, Nancy would open the front door where she would find a basket of well wishes in the form of a casserole, meal, or perhaps a dessert. Her heart was touched by the gestures of kindness, but her grief left her empty of hunger. She found herself packaging the meals and sweets into containers and placing them in the freezer. This pattern became a familiar routine... until one day something changed.

Nancy opened her front door to something unusual, yet strangely familiar. It wasn't a meal, casserole, or dessert, but rather grocery bags overflowing with treasures. These bags contained everything she needed and a few things more! Someone who understood her struggle had anticipated Nancy's needs before Nancy even knew what she needed. The bags were filled with things like napkins, tissues, paper towels, toilet paper, plastic bags, wraps, toothpaste etc. It included everything she would have included on a grocery list had she been able to think that far ahead. It was chock-full of both essentials for her home and essentials for her heart. This message of hope came in a most unconventional way, but it came just the same. Perhaps the slight humor it caused and the coincidence it served up made its way to ping her brokenness and begin mending the still-fragile wounds. Healing takes time, and this gift allowed

Nancy an extended time to shelter at home before braving a public trip to the grocery store.

When I first asked Nancy if I could interview her, she shared with me that she felt she could not be of much help for this particular book. She knew I was looking for parents who prayed their children through circumstances, and she believed she fell short of that essential requirement. She explained that in the days following the tragedy of 9/11, she could not pray. She didn't know where to start nor what to ask for, other than a prayer that her husband would somehow walk through the front door. God knew Nancy, and Nancy knew God, and He did not abandon her when she needed him most for the Holy Spirit *"itself interceded with inexpressible groanings,"* calling for hope, healing and, yes, even a grocery bag filled with essentials!

We cannot always see the graces as they pour from the sky and all the channels they go through before they arrive at their final destination, but we know from where they originated. God loves his children and is faithful to them. Sometimes, we just need to let the Holy Spirit take our thoughts and carry them to the heart of Jesus, for we do not always know how to pray as we ought.

What is so interesting about this story is how the Holy Spirit guides and instructs each of us to deliver His heavenly hope to a world of darkness. The person who took the time to shop for Nancy did not simply fill some bags with essentials but rather took the time to enter into her sorrow and contemplate her needs. By opening ourselves up to the Holy Spirit, we can feel the prompting and act accordingly (and ever so timely) to deliver divine packages. Nancy admits that many gifts of hope were sent her way by means of cards, meals, calls, thoughtful words, and prayers. For some reason, the sack of groceries or the timing of it at her doorway became the lens that brought every other gift into focus. Those many bright rays of hope led her through, and eventually away from, the darkness of her sorrow.

One of many lessons I took away from my time with Nancy is to always be obedient to the inspiration to act. You never know how much your small light may mean to the one who sits in despair and is surrounded by darkness.

Breaking the Silence, Restoring "Our" Family

Dear God,

That morning changed everything. You knew of this day before the day even came. You knew that September 11, 2001, would be a day of intense prayer and crying out to The Almighty. You knew how much we would need You on that day.

I was one of many who mourned a loss, pleading for an answer, a reason… a reversal. I didn't want my children to grow up without their father, and it crushed me to imagine raising our children alone. I begged You to please let this be a nightmare that I could and would soon wake from.

In the days after, I did not know what to pray. Forgive me for my silence, but I simply had no words. A fog of hopelessness, despair, and heartache filled my soul. You were patient with me as the Holy Spirit perfected my thoughts and needs into prayers; prayers you answered in wondrous ways.

You sent our family letters of sympathy and letters of hope. You sent us meals, money, and even groceries. You knew what we needed, and You worked through the hands and feet of Your warriors to bless us, touch us, and hold us. We could not have moved if it had not been for Your faithful servants. Through them, we saw Your face and remembered Your love.

Is Your grace not sufficient? I feel You carrying us through this. We feel the presence of Dennis as he urges his family to carry on. I feel his strength and wisdom in every decision I make for our children. How is it that loss can be gain, that less can be more, that sorrow can bring joy?

From the day I became his wife, there were three of us—Dennis and me and You in the center of everything. Now it is down to just You and me! I trust we can do it. I trust this is still a strong team. Gather "our" children upon Your Almighty lap when they are overwhelmed. Hear the prayers they dare not say aloud and the feelings they cannot even put into words. Creator of man, Father to all, please bless us with Your mercy when we mourn. In Christ Jesus' name, we pray, Amen.

This prayer was inspired by the interview with Nancy Moroney and is dedicated to the loving memory of her husband, Dennis Gerard Moroney: November 7, 1961 – September 11, 2001. Dennis' memorial at the 9/11 museum in New York City can be found at the North Pool, position N-47, among so many others who lost their lives that day.

Prayer Prompt

Have you ever felt as Nancy did, when she could not muster the strength nor the words to offer a prayer from the depth of her sorrowful soul? Try opening your heart and mind to the Holy Spirit whoever so gently envelops those in need. As gentle as a breeze brushes by your skin or through your hair, so too the Holy Spirit surrounds and enters His child's soul. Invite the Holy Spirit into your day and look for Him to reveal Himself to your family directly or through the holy ones around you.

Meditation Prayer for a Sorrowful Parent and Child Who Have Lost a Loved One

I know You experience the death of Your children each day, Dear Lord. We feel You weeping with us because of our loss, but we also know, at the same time, You are able to rejoice with [name of deceased parent], for another one of Your children has returned to You. When we close our eyes, we can imagine the joy it must bring to [name of deceased parent] to be in Your Almighty Presence. Although we miss [him/her] very much, we could never wish for [his/her] return to Earth because it would mean having to leave the eternal dwelling You have graciously prepared for Your loving servant. Instead, we ask [his/her] soul to continue to pray for us from above and to await the day we too can join [him/her] in Heaven with You, the glorious saints, and the angelic choirs.

Help me find a way to be an effective and loving single parent, as it is painful here without [her/his] help, love, and constant support. I feel incomplete when I try to parent alone, with half the words, half the gifts, half the perspective, and half the love. All-powerful God, through Your providential outpouring of care, please complete me.

You created us in Your image to be your sons and daughters, and You love us with a kind of love we do not yet fully understand, for Your love is like the burning sun that singularly lights the world. Therefore, dear Lord, since Your love is so pure and so true, let but a ray of it shine into our hearts and heal the sorrow we now feel. Allow Your ray of hope to burst forth, from our most tender and sorrowful souls to others, so they too might know and love You through our redemptive suffering.*

Please help my child grow in faith, love, and charity. Allow [him/her] special insight and understanding into Your holy ways, so Your will might be accomplished within [his/her] soul. We invite You into our home to teach us, mold us, and protect us. Please send Your Holy Spirit to envelop us, fill us, and seal us with Your goodness and love. May we also ask, dear Lord, that You brighten our days with sweet memories and vivid thoughts of the one we lost. We wish, as a family, to continue to honor and praise the life of [name of deceased parent]. With a joyful heart, we graciously cherish the gift of time we each spent knowing and loving [him/her]. Amen.

*Redemptive Suffering — You may have heard the term "offer it up." Actually, throughout the ages, many saints have taught us about the power of redemptive suffering. Redemptive suffering occurs when a person chooses to direct their current or ongoing suffering (pain, hardship, sorrow, a debilitating cross, etc.) to God through prayer for His use in the redemption of His people. In this way, and because of our free will, we are able to offer such earthly sufferings or sacrifices back to the Father God, as Jesus did from the cross, so that no sufferings are wasted but instead are used to glorify His Heavenly Kingdom. Each of us are given crosses to bear and are asked by Jesus to deny ourselves, take up our cross daily, and follow him (cf, Luke 9:23). St. Paul told the Colossians that he rejoiced in his own suffering (cf, Col 1:24). The saints teach us that our suffering, united to Jesus, allows us to experience a profound intimacy with our Savior as we share in His ongoing work to bring souls to Heaven.

Praying Your Child Through Anything
...Even a Severely Impaired Mind and Body

Rather, God chose the foolish of the world to shame the wise, and God chose the weak of the world to shame the strong, and God chose the lowly and despised of the world, those who count for nothing, to reduce to nothing those who are something, so that no human being might boast before God.
1 Corinthians 1:27-29

"You have to meet Lisa and Michael," was all I heard for weeks from a few of my friends who knew I was writing this prayer book. They were right— this couple is amazing! I learned so much from our talk, not just about Christopher, their adopted son, but about the parents who took him into their home with eyes wide open to his inherent challenges. Lisa and Michael wanted to give him a life he might not otherwise have, and they answered the call to put their lives on hold to adopt a son who would demand everything they had to give.

Christopher suffered from numerous debilitating conditions and was expected by all doctors' accounts to live no longer than a few years, if he even made it that far. He never was able to talk and never had the strength to walk, so he was fully dependent on those around him for his life. What his parents offered in continuous care was returned to them in graces tenfold. The loving care Christopher received, along with the outpouring of blessings from God, offered him several years past his diagnosed life expectancy. Christopher actually experienced his tenth, twentieth, and even thirtieth birthdays before dying only a few weeks before his thirty-first year was completed.

It was not easy to watch their son struggle, and they wanted so much more for him. The pain-filled days were especially difficult. Some days, they confessed, were spent in anger toward God, trying to make sense of why this child could not have a day of freedom from the feeble frame and muddled mind that held him hostage. Other days were downright exhausting, and they wondered if they were capable of the patience and energy needed to visit yet another doctor. They would pray for pain-free days and even a way to trade places with him who suffered greatly. Despite the pain, the suffering, and the challenges—Christopher always found peace and loved his nightly prayer to God.

Lisa shared a most intimate story about her husband Michael, who was dressing eight-year-old Christopher for Sunday Mass on Father's Day when his son began a severe grand mal seizure— one that his father knew could take his life. Michael cradled Christopher in his arms and called for immediate assistance from the Creator. His prayer was one of desperation as he pleaded for another day to share with his son and asked God to please not take Christopher yet.

The loving father also prayed for the dreadful episode to leave his son and for the suffering to end. Michael did not know the answer to his prayer immediately but continued to thank God for the son he rocked and cradled in his arms. Lisa said the room was thick with God's presence that morning, as if together, his earthly and Heavenly Father were holding onto Christopher. She described it as if Heaven had swooped down and enveloped them into a celestial realm, keeping them safe while they waited for the paramedics to arrive. Eventually, with the help of the medical team, the suffering subsided. His wracked body became still and calm once more. God had granted Michael, a most humble and earnest servant, his dire request for another day with Christopher. At least today, on Father's Day, he would not have to give his son back to God.

Although Christopher spoke few words, his parents said they knew him intimately. His quiet nature enabled them to look into his soul for communication, and they found themselves opening their own vulnerable souls back to him. They talked and communicated on a deeper level than any other human being they had known. Christopher watched his parents and learned their behaviors. He truly absorbed their love and returned love back to them.

Lisa and Michael took Christopher everywhere they went. Catholic Mass was a favorite outing. They were convinced Christopher understood God's presence, as he would act so reverently during the consecration, when the priest would change ordinary bread and wine into the Body and Blood of Jesus Christ. Christopher would raise his eyes and hands toward the altar and onward to heaven as if he truly was participating in something celestial. Christopher's sincere gestures would remind all those around him not to take for granted the precious miracle taking place at Mass. How is it that one who cannot speak, teaches; and one who cannot even write his name, composes volumes upon our hearts?

If you ask Michael and Lisa, they would tell you that it was their honor and blessing to be the parents of Christopher. They would admit that the cross was very heavy at times but also sweet and purposeful. They would share that they never felt closer to God than through the son who captured their hearts and changed their lives forever.

Bearer of Christ

Dear Almighty and Wondrous Creator,

You do NOT make mistakes. We hear it often said, but to live it, gives new meaning and depth to your perfect plan. We look across the fields of heather as they stand straight, their contrast beautiful against the cobalt sky. We watch as the stems bend in unison with the gentleness of the breeze. Its beauty is both uniform and individual. Then we glimpse a brightness growing within the field, and it looks alone and is unfamiliar from the rest. How did such a seed find rest on this earth, and what is its purpose? We are attracted to its glow and difference, and it calls to us to come closer. A wildflower of great beauty has been sewn among the field, perhaps dropped by a bird…or maybe a dove.

The beautiful wildflower had a name; it was Christopher (Bearer of Christ), your unique and perfect creation. What he lacked in the physical and mental realms was to be exceeded by unconventional wisdom and joy. Earthly predictions said he would not bloom for long. However, this precious wildflower, found within the bouquet of humanity, continues to spread his fragrance of love everywhere.

We both came to trust You more through Christopher for, in reality, to whom else shall we go? So faithfully were You there for us as we walked through life and even near-death moments with our son. Oh, how we cried for You to allow us another day with him, and then another, because the loss of him would mean a loss of our portal to heaven from Earth. Your ways became our ways, Your will became our will, and we were blessed with an amazing thirty-year journey with the companionship of our son.

Without Christopher, our hearts have an emptiness only You can fill. We miss him. We know you granted us additional playtime—perhaps we all needed it! Thank you for the joy of knowing him and the opportunity to be his parents. His flower never fades, and we think of him often when we wander through the field, especially when we are lucky enough to spot another Christopher in bloom.

We will close with the simple prayer our family prayed each night with Christopher. "Dear Jesus, please bless and protect Christopher and keep him from harm. We love him very much. Amen."

Thank you, God, for the cross You lovingly placed before us, for the courage to pick it up, and for the numerous graces that flowed from it, Amen.

This prayer was inspired by the interview with Michael and Lisa Patchner, Indianapolis, IN. This prayer is dedicated to the loving memory of Christopher Michael Patchner 4/6/1983 – 3/18/2014.

Prayer Prompt

*God's miracles are all around us. Pray for heavenly eyes:
to see not as the world sees, but as God sees.*

Meditation Prayer for a Parent Who Has a Child With a Special Need

Dear Most Holy Lord God,

Thank You for the wildflowers among the fields of heather and for the single flame of candlelight that dispels the darkness. Thank You for the single shiny penny dropped and forgotten by one but spotted and treasured by another. Thank You for the one hovering cloud that affords us relief from the scorching sun. You always know what we need and from Your abundant love poured forth our special child, [name].

We pray that [he/she] understands how much [he/she] means to us and what a treasure we find in each day we spend together. Create in me a Spirit to love, as You would desire for me to love [him/her]. Humble me so I may learn as well as teach, uncovering the hidden gifts of my child's purpose. Allow me to serve [name] as I would serve You with a humble and compassionate heart. May [he/she] see Your tender eyes through mine to know the intenseness of my love, for I am already blessed with the presence of You within [him/her]. Amen.

Praying Your Child Through Anything
...Even a Most Humbling Miracle

"... Father, if you are willing, take this cup away from me; still, not my will but yours be done." [And to strengthen him, an angel from heaven appeared to him. He was in such agony, and he prayed so fervently that his sweat became like drops of blood falling on the ground.] Luke 22:42-44

Yes, sometimes, God takes the cup away. For it is His will that we first view the cup in all its potential horror only to be removed before we must taste its bitterness or drink its poison. Miracles are like that. Although some remain subtle, others are most deliberate and leave us without doubt that divine intervention has been at play in our lives. That was the case in this next story of a humbling miracle and the family who lived their day in the Garden of Gethsemane. Only this time, God chose to remove the cup before it even touched their lips.

Annabelle was three years old, playing outside with her older brother (Will) and a neighborhood friend of her brother's. Annabelle had just recently earned her wings, so to speak. At age three, she was finally allowed to spend some time with her brother and his friend outside without the constant supervision of her cautious mother. It was late afternoon, and Annabelle's mom (Danielle) was prepping dinner while her dad (Brian) was out for a bike ride. As Brian approached their home on his return, he noticed the three children playing an odd game in the driveway. Instead of simply tossing the ball to each other to see how high or how far they could throw, they upped the ante to include an obstacle—the peaked roof covering the front porch.

One boy would stand on one side of the covered porch, and the other would try to throw the ball high enough to clear the peak and have its momentum safely drive the ball over into the hands of the catcher. Brian immediately saw the lack of wisdom in this little game and tried to convince them to try another ball game, but they were laughing and having such a great time that he decided to leave them with only a warning. "Okay, guys, play your game, but if the ball gets stuck on the roof, and I am confident it will very soon, then the game is over. Got it?" With all fun resumed, Brian went into the house to find Danielle in the kitchen.

The Miracle

It was not long after the warning that they heard the footsteps of two children running up the stairs to the second level. Curious, but still just in wondering mode, they perked up to listen for more. Only one child descended the stairs, and it was the neighbor boy. "Annabelle fell out of the window; Annabelle fell out of the window!"

Still not understanding what all of this meant, they remember thinking she was still outside and perhaps had gotten into one of the cars and slipped out a window. Nothing made sense until… it did. Following the neighbor boy outside, they saw that a window screen had fallen from their second-story master bedroom onto the cement driveway. Then they saw Annabelle, who had just moments before accompanied the window screen on the fifteen-foot journey down to the unforgiving cement slab. Her brother was right next to her and calling her name. "Belle, are you okay? Oh, Belle, are you hurt?"

After dismissing the neighbor boy, the family got to work. The first call was for an ambulance. It all went quickly from there. The paramedics loaded Annabelle and Danielle into the emergency vehicle for the trip to the hospital, and Brian drove Will in the car to meet them. After a full examination, the prognosis was in— Annabelle had a small scrape on her arm from coming in contact with the porch rooftop. That was it! No other scrape, bump, bruise, or sign of a problem. Yet, of course, the parents were told to be on close watch for the next few days and nights as any internal damage would reveal itself through swelling, concussion, or unexplained pains.

That night and for the next few, sweet Annabelle slept between mom and dad. Will got to join the slumber party with a prime position on the floor right next to their bed. It was a time to be together. It was a time for closeness and thankfulness. It was a time for prayer and gratitude. But it was also a time of nightmares and high tension as the "what ifs" kept playing out in their minds, only to have them wake again to the unharmed child sleeping peacefully beside them.

Before and After

Both Brian and Danielle were prayerful before the accident. Both sought the will of God in their lives and covered their children in prayer each day. After Annabelle's fall, they both experienced an even richer, more profound, and deeper faith. They said that it was a defining moment and solidified for them that *they are not the ones in control!* Leaning even more heavily into God's Providence, they now understand clearly their roles as a team member, albeit an important position, but definitely with God as their coach and protector. When asked if they could give me a glimpse of how they pray now for Will and Annabelle, they both were eager to share. Although their prayers differed in words, the message was consistent. "We can't imagine trying to raise children without our faith. Prayer gives us perspective and keeps us grounded."

Danielle often feels called to pray for deep rest for their bodies and souls, allowing their hearts and minds to recover from one day and possess the vitality to start a new one. She loves the God-given freedom and energy found in "new beginnings" and shares her passion with her children through prayer. Among other things, she also prays for God to guide their hearts and minds, to give them peace, and to help them be kind. She prays for good friendships for her children and for them to be worthy friends to others.

Brian claimed that his prayer has evolved over time, and he adds words to it as needed, but that he has committed to memory a collection of thoughts that were inspired through his own prayer life. As the words flowed from his mouth, I couldn't even write, they were so touching and real. I had him repeat it again so I could capture its natural beauty. Here is Brian's heartfelt prayer, offered to God each day as his children get out of the car and head into school:

"Lord, watch over my kids today. Give them your strength, courage, love and wisdom, kindness, and discernment. Give them the strength and courage to do what is right, even when it is hard and even when they don't want to. Shroud the school with your safety, Amen."

Reflecting on the Fall

What is so odd, too, is that Annabelle remembers only looking from the window to try to see the ball. The next thing she remembers is waking up on the ground. She does not remember the sensation or fear of falling. In fact, she remembers wondering how she suddenly appeared on the driveway. Annabelle suffered no other issues, and the small scrape healed quickly. To look at the family a week later, they would look exactly the way they did the week before the accident/miracle. But if you could peek inside, you would see the brilliant scars of a miracle etched into their hearts and souls. A miracle has a way of changing us forever.

Perhaps it is the humility that is stirred in the one who receives such a Divine gift as a miracle, for the gift is so personally tailored to fit only one immediate need, as if it were monogrammed in Heaven with her full name, address, and social security number! Miracles are so perfectly designed and created for their specific purpose that it could fit no other than the one it was intended for. And…it always arrives at the perfect time!

It is through our love for each other that we share in the treasure of the miracles God sends forth. The light of just one miracle is far-reaching and intense because it is Providentially energized. Its effects last through many lifetimes, only to be retold for generations to come. Oh, what a wondrous God we have Who sends us these beautiful miracles of hope.

A Prayer of Utter Thanksgiving

Oh, Most Merciful and Gracious Father,

Words cannot begin to show our gratitude to You for the miracle You showered upon us. Undeserving as we are, You still reached out to provide us with a message of hope and love. Your mighty miracle was not lost on us, and we have grown even closer to You through the mystery. What baffles us is that we did not even know to pray because we did not even know there was danger. You took care of things before we even realized what had happened. And even after we knew, the heaven-sent marvel still did not completely compute in our minds. What an awesome God of timeless wonder You are.

What if the miracle had not come? Sometimes, dear heavenly Father, our minds grow restless as we reflect on that day and begin to imagine worse outcomes. We beg You to transform all of our "what ifs" into the more constructive question of "what now?" Remind us to ask often, "what now, my Lord, what now?" Annabelle has been spared for Your purpose, dear God. Whatever it might be, please help us best prepare her for the future You created her for. We ask your angels, who gathered on that day to break her fall, to continue to watch over Annabelle, guiding her always on the pathway to Heaven.

Your miracle has forever changed the trajectory of our lives. As even the smallest profound statement can impact a desire for changes in our life, so much more is a profound miracle when the veil from Heaven is lifted before our very eyes. Just as you summoned the angel to the aid of Your Son in the Garden of Gethsemane, you again directed the angelic host to tend to your servant Annabelle and her family. We must remember that soon after our Lord Jesus felt the soothing comfort and strength from heaven, through those glorious moments of relief, he still went on to pick up His cross. Being spared, comforted, or healed is not a hall pass through life, and this miracle blessing is not lost on us as her parents. We will never be able to begin to repay you for the blessings you have showered on us, Oh God, but we will joyfully spend our lives beholden to You and Your will for our family. Amen.

This prayer was inspired by the interview with Brian and Danielle Heit of Steamboat Springs, Colorado.

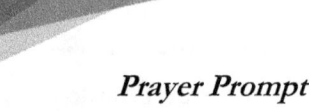

Prayer Prompt

"... I have neither silver nor gold, but what I do have I give you: in the name of Jesus Christ the Nazorean, [rise and] walk. Then Peter took him by the right hand and raised him up, and immediately his feet and ankles grew strong. He leaped up, stood, and walked around, and went into the temple with them, walking and jumping and praising God." Acts 3: 6-8

Meditation Prayer for Parents Who Are Humbled by a Miracle

Dear God,

Wow, where did that come from? Oh, the miracles You send into my life and into the life of my child! Thank You, thank You, thank You. They bring such happiness to our world.

Open my eyes to their humble teachings. Do not let us miss Your messages of love nor cast them off as coincidences. Allow us to forever remain childlike in our enthusiasm for Your heavenly presents, unwrapping each with gusto and great joy. Help us acknowledge, with celestial delight, the moment when Your almighty command placed the unmerited miracle in motion, and Your omnipotence delivered it to my child.

Please help us to breathe in the fragrance of the miracle You created and sent forth, marked specifically for my child. So personal a gift that You sent, so personal the prayer that flows back to You in thanksgiving. Holy Spirit, please perfect my prayer and make it pleasing and fitting for the Almighty One, who desired to bestow such a favor upon my child. In Jesus' name, I ask all of these things. Amen.

Praying Your Child Through Anything
...Even a Call to the Priesthood

When he disembarked and saw the vast crowd, his heart was moved with pity for them, for they were like sheep without a shepherd; and he began to teach them many things. Mark 6:34

I had the pleasure to meet a most prayerful and beautiful woman named Fe. She may be petite in stature, but she is mighty. She is mighty in holiness, virtue, praise, and song—as she can belt it out like an opera star! But it was her meekness and humility that drew me in, and she was kind and attentive to everyone she met.

It was during our talks that I would hear some great stories about her son, the internationally-known priest/famous chef/best-selling author/radio host/television host/black belt martial arts instructor/breakdance choreographer... and the list continues. It is exhausting just thinking about his many accomplishments. Fe is the mother of Fr. Leo Patalinghug, a shepherding priest who is attracting a multitude of faithful followers on the journey toward Christ.

A mother shares more about her son's character than he would ever tell about himself. A mother sees her son through a multitude of lenses. Her perspective scans from the cradle to the present including; wins, losses, sufferings, insecurities, infatuations, friends, choices, and accomplishments that all contribute to building a child's unique personality. These important steps are not lost on a mother who watches her child grow day-by-day and year-by-year. Fe instilled faith in her young children and believes that God molds and forms each of us in the innocence and pliability of childhood, while we are most receptive to His important virtues, values, and characteristics. Children may not exercise this faith for years, but the seed remains planted and is at the core of who they are.

Fe shared a few stories with me about Fr. Leo that she believes led him to the priesthood. If you are a mom or dad who desires your son or daughter to serve God in a religious way, take notice of the intimate prayers of Fe. She desires only to please God, taking her queues and lessons of faith from all the holy ones who came before her.

Growing up in the Patalinghug Family

Fe and Carlos loved the Lord God and raised each of their four children to honor and know the Trinity of God Father, God in Jesus Christ, our Savior, and in God the Holy Spirit. They both were open to one or more of their children accepting the call to a religious vocation, but Fe privately prayed for one of her two sons to be called to the priesthood. She had a great respect for priests throughout her life and felt it would be an honor and privilege to parent a future priest for God's people. Through a daily consecration prayer to Jesus through Mary, she would imagine placing each child in the palm of her hands and lifting them up to God, offering and surrendering them to His will in their lives.

Carlos Patalinghug was a physician in the Philippines while their first three children grew. It was a poor town where he practiced medicine, and Carlos was often paid in chickens or produce for his medical services. The family enjoyed many luxuries and employed five servants to cook and clean for them. Fe wanted for nothing; food was prepared, children were looked after, drivers were designated (she had no driver's license), and even her toothbrush was loaded and ready at her sink before each bedtime! Her life was good, and she loved God, her husband, and her children. Fe was a teacher in their town and enjoyed working with and getting to know the families and the children. Teaching was her way to offer something back to the town she loved and cared for. Their fourth child was born in 1970, and they named him Leo after the thirteen "Leo" Popes who spanned from St. Leo I, aka St. Leo the Great who was elected pope in the year 440 to St. Leo XIII ending his papacy in the year 1903.

Soon after Leo was born, Carlos was offered an opportunity to practice medicine in the United States. There were many pros and cons to moving the family, but ultimately, they decided it was best for them to accept this challenge. It came with many difficult trade-offs. The move would prove to be a difficult adjustment for Fe, as she would no longer have help around the home and for their four young children. Carlos left immediately for the U.S. to complete the necessary studies required for the transition while Fe prepared the rest of the household for departure.

For Fe, those months alone in the Philippines and again at the onset of life in the U.S.A. would be especially trying. Fe and the children made the move to reunite with Carlos when their oldest child was nine years old, and the youngest child, Leo, was only twenty months old. When Carlos wasn't studying, he was working to provide as much as he could for his family. The first home he was able to secure in the United States was meager and filled with cockroaches. God was calling them to a new way of living, stripping them of the comforts they had come to know but also opening the family up to a new country with many possibilities.

While the older children attended school, Fe and Leo immersed themselves in quality time together, and they formed a tight bond as she shared her many chores and her numerous prayers with her small boy. It was a blessing she had not been afforded in the Philippians, with her busy teaching schedule and the house staff tending to the children. Each night, after dinner, Fe would take the four children up to her bedroom, where she had constructed a small altar on top of her dresser. There they would kneel to pray the Rosary* together, and with every other decade, they would pray with outstretched arms. Little Leo would cling to his mother's leg, and many times, he would fall fast asleep while the others prayed. By the age of four, little Leo would gladly join in praying decades of the Rosary with outstretched arms like Jesus on the Cross.

Leo grew into a teenager and was into designer clothes, cute girls, and music. His faith would waver between hot and cold. Mass was not his thing. In fact, he found it boring and looked for excuses to not have to attend. There were times Fe would have to use a cold, wet cloth to wake him up from falling asleep during the church services. She was feisty and demanded results.

A Trip, a Miracle, and a Calling

Fe was silent about her prayers that Leo would someday desire to be a priest. She and Carlos taught each of their children how to work hard for what they wanted. They trusted their children and allowed them freedom to choose their own paths. Carlos and Fe used prayer to help guide them toward the will of God. One summer, during Leo's college years, Fe was handed a flyer about the amazing miracles and apparitions of Our Blessed Mother in a small quaint town in the countries of Bosnia and Herzegovina. She showed the pamphlet on Medjugorje to her eldest son (also named Carlos) to gauge his interest. Carlos was a very devout young man and was immediately drawn to the chance to visit such a holy place. Carlos shared the adventure with his two sisters, Maria and Angelica, and they also decided to go. That left Leo— either he would join in on the pilgrimage with his siblings, or he would stay back with mom and dad. Leo was not the least bit excited about this kind of trip but, like any kid not wanting to be left out, decided to go rather than stay at home.

Off the four Patalinghug children went on a pilgrimage to Medjugorje. While there, Leo's older brother remembers seeing a strange sight. Leo was standing in the corner of the large church with his hands covering his ears and his feet kicking in protest—yet there was no one around him. There was not a soul within earshot as Leo stood alone, fighting an invisible force. Leo would not share the battle that he fought while in Medjugorje until he himself was ready to accept the outcome.

Medjugorje made quite an impact on the family children, and they deeply desired to bring home something beautiful and meaningful to their parents. Too heavy to pack in a suitcase, they hand-carried a large statuette of Our Blessed Mother with them on the plane.

Once home, they offered the gift to Fe, who loved and treasured such a beautiful sentiment from her children. They could have easily brought back a packable book, a pocket-sized rosary, or any number of trinkets for sale. But no, they chose a heavy sculpture of Mary! The sacrifices her children made to haul this piece home safely were amazing to her. The next morning Fe rose early and looked at the beautiful figure of the Blessed Mother, pondering a place of honor Our Lady deserved in their home. She decided the mantle above the fireplace would be the perfect setting. The statuette was so heavy that to reach the mantle, it made hoisting it a bit difficult and awkward, but Fe steadied her hands as she settled the beautiful woman into place. Taking a step back to admire the wonderful gift from her children, Fe noticed something very peculiar. The scent of roses filled the room. She looked around to see if someone had entered behind her carrying a huge bouquet, but there was no one else around. Fe was elated upon remembering this beautiful scent is a heavenly gift and has, for centuries, denoted the miraculous presence of Mary to many pilgrims, saints, and people in need. This statuette would prove to be even more special in the ensuing years as visitors will often receive the fragrant gift of roses as they gather in the Patalinghug home.

Leo graduated from college with a political science degree and was contemplating law school. Fe and Carlos often asked Leo, "What are you going to do with your life, son?" Leo was unsure and consistently waved off their question, saying he was working on it. The truth was, he had never quite found the perfect fit.

Having graduated from college and more than a year after they returned from Medjugorje, Leo climbed the stairs of their home and began calling out to his mom from the hallway, "Mom, can I talk to you?" She expected that he needed some money or her help with something. Telling him where he could find her, he entered the bedroom and asked her to sit down. Then he dropped the *heavenly* bomb— "You know how you and dad are always asking me what I am going to do with my life? Well, I have decided on something. I am going to practice a celibate life, and I am going to look into the priesthood." Fe screamed with great joy, threw her hands up in praise to God, and peace filled her heart. Her prayer had been answered! Leo hesitated and firmly reminded his mom that he was not a priest yet and that many years of discernment were necessary to get to that level. Fe didn't worry about the waiting nor the discerning. She believed it was, indeed, the will of God that Leo would open his heart to the priesthood. What joy filled their home that day!

Fe confided in Leo about her long-standing secret prayer for him and her consecration of all of her children to God through the Blessed Mother Mary. She told him it was he who especially penetrated her heart as she prayed earnestly for his calling, if it were to be the will of God.

Leo then confided to his mother about the message and miracles he received in Medjugorje. In the corner of the church when he was completely alone, he heard the sweet calling from the Blessed Mother. The heavenly voice, he had so fiercely resisted at first, had actually come to bring fulfillment and peace to a searching soul. He found his path within Mary's invitation. She had told Leo, loud and clear, she desired him to become a priest.

The passing of time has not diminished Fe's reaction to this life-changing news for, as she recounted the story during our interview, tears of joy filled her eyes. Answered prayers, especially when they take decades to mature, are often so personal and intimate that they renew the grace within us as often as we are willing to share the story with others.

The following are two prayers that were inspired by Fe. One is directed to God the Father, while the second is requesting the intercession of Mary, the Blessed Mother. God chose Mary's pure womb to deliver His son into the world. With very special graces, He allowed human parents to raise the Savior of the World. Why do you think God chose to send His only begotten Son to Earth in this manner? We believe this Holy Family serves as a model for us. We can learn and grow in holiness by imitating St. Joseph and Mary. We believe saints in heaven never stop praying, especially for us still struggling on Earth. A powerful way to infuse special graces and holiness into our families is to appeal to St. Joseph and Mary for their intercessory prayers to God on our behalf.

A Prayer to Answer a Heavenly Call
And
A Mom-to-Mom Request

Dear Eternal Father,

You have blessed us with children, and I desire to please You. I petition, on behalf of our family, to make us Yours and to use us to grow and fortify Your kingdom. Let Your will fill our souls with direction and a yearning and desire to love You, share You, and protect Your honor.

Humbly I give You my life and the lives of my children, surrendering all to Your will in our lives. Allow the Truth of Your Son to penetrate our hearts, our lives, and our entire beings so that we may shine Your light everywhere you ask us to be.

If it is Your will, dear Heavenly Father, call upon my children to serve You in a special way. If it be Your will that even one of our boys should become a priest, I will imitate Our Blessed Mother and pray for my son daily, supporting his efforts and ministry in whatever ways I can as long as I shall live.

Finally, dear Lord, please bless me with the patience to trust Your timing and to remember that You are in control, not me. Amen.

Dear Mama Mary,

I speak to you mother-to-mother and ask for your intercession that, like your holy family, our family might also yearn to please God and be used to build His mighty kingdom. In following your humble example, "let it (also) be done to me according to His will." You answered yes to the angel Gabriel, and I also offer my 'YES" on behalf of the family God has entrusted to me. Help me raise children who will love you, honor you, and propagate the Good News of your Divine Son to the world around them.

I offer you my contrite heart in hopes you will mold it into the beauty of your perfect human heart, which beat only with love for God. The abundant and overflowing graces of God flow through you to soothe your poor and hungry children. Feed us then, not what we deserve, but what your motherly ardor desires us to have. With your maternal love, please sweeten the crosses we must bear and remind us often of the heaviest cross your Son chose to recompense our sinfulness and purchase our salvation.

Heavenly Mother, please guide me on the path of your Son, your Holy Spouse, and your Heavenly Father that I should know, without doubt, I am where I am needed. Through your precious Son's name, we pray, Amen.

The above prayers were inspired by the interview with Mrs. Fe Patalinghug.

Father Leo Patalinghug biography (just read what prayers can do!)

Yes, Fr. Leo is a Catholic priest—but that is not all! Fr. Leo Patalinghug is a priest member of a community of consecrated life, *Voluntas Dei* (The Will of God). He is the creator and founder of an international food and faith movement called Plating Grace and founder and chair of the nonprofit group The Table Foundation. He is a best-selling author, acclaimed international speaker, host for radio, podcast, and a weekly international food and faith show on EWTN, *Savoring our Faith*. His unique background as a chef and his previous experience as a two-time blackbelt martial arts instructor and former award-winning break-dancer and choreographer has earned the attention of major media outlets, including The Food Network where he won "Throwdown with Bobby Flay!" The mission to see food as a gift from God to nourish your family and to strengthen relationships is making this world a better place one meal at a time.

A little more on Fe:

Dr. Patalinghug and Fe return to Cataingan in the Province of Masbate, Philippines, each year to bring much-needed food and medical supplies (and a huge dose of faith) to the people in the village where they lived. They spend time seeing patients and talking to them about their struggles and their blessings. In 1995, The Patalinghug family erected a forty-foot cross, high upon a hill, to watch over the town and the sea. It took seven people to build it out of concrete and another fifty people to carry it and mount it into place. Many hands and hearts were needed to plan, create, build, transport, position, reinforce, secure, and erect this monumental cross. God honors and blesses our individual efforts and sacrifices, but he will especially honor the harmonious efforts of a town that desires to acknowledge God in this spectacular way. Fishermen have said the cross has glowed at night, bringing them peace and guidance home. Townspeople have found comfort and their own safety since the cross has been erected. Added in 2018 on a path leading upward to the cross are the fourteen Stations of the Cross. The hill is a beautiful place of prayer and contemplation as God watches over the humble townspeople and the farmland and sea that help sustain them. It has become a pilgrimage site for many and serves as a reminder that this family, no matter where they may be, will forever cover this town and its beautiful people in prayer.

*Rosary: The Rosary is a powerful traditional prayer, using a strand of beads that are designed in a particular order to honor God through the Blessed Virgin Mary. Through the five decades, one contemplates the life of Christ in what are called Mysteries of the faith. It is believed that the cadence and rhythm of this devotion are soothing and enlightening to those who pray it and also awards those who pray it in earnest with special graces from God.

When praying the daily Rosary*, Fe dedicates the second mystery to her son, Fr. Leo, and to all priests and religious. She graciously agreed to share her beautiful prayer with us:

May the angels of God safely bring him to his ministry, wherever he is called to be of service.
May the Blessed Mother gather him under her protective mantle and shield him from evil.
May the Holy Spirit impart wisdom into his soul that he should speak boldly the Word of God.
May he be given both strength and gentleness to lift souls up to you and to open their hearts to your graces and mercy.
May you encourage, inspire, and lead more young men and women to holiness and the ministries that will proclaim the Good News of Christ, our Savior.
May you bless all families to pray together and for each other as they keep your Holy Name sacred and revered for all generations.

I petition for these gifts through your Son, Jesus Christ, Amen.

Prayer Prompt

God answers prayers! Do you know someone who would make a wonderful priest or who is contemplating the religious life?
If so, sincerely place them on your heart as you:
- *Contemplate their values, virtues, and gifts as well as the inherent struggles, hurdles, and rivalry that come with leading a holy life.*
- *Offer your candidate up to God for His will to be done through him or her, and ask God to guide you in daily prayer for this person.*
- *Consider requesting a special spiritual gift or blessing for them each day.*

Meditation Prayer to Consecrate a Child to a Holy or Religious Life

Dear Almighty Creator and Giver of Blessings,

You have placed on my heart a candidate for religious life. I now lift them up to You and promise I will pray for their holiness throughout my life. Your will be done through them, not mine. I ask only that You use these prayers for the continued protection, strength, and vitality of Your holy Church on Earth. Accept this prayer from Your humble and contrite servant and bless me with a clear understanding for the gifts You desire me to pray for on their behalf so they may, for Your glory alone, live a fruitful and fulfilling life. May they, through their ministry, bring many souls closer to You. Amen.

Praying Your Child Through Anything
...Even From Lost to a Leader

Finally, draw your strength from the Lord and from his mighty power. Put on the armor of God so that you may be able to stand firm against the tactics of the devil. For our struggle is not with flesh and blood but with the principalities, with the powers, with the world rulers of this present darkness, with the evil spirits in the heavens. Therefore, put on the armor of God, that you may be able to resist on the evil day and, having done everything, to hold your ground. So stand fast with your loins girded in truth, clothed with righteousness as a breastplate, and your feet shod in readiness for the gospel of peace. In all circumstances, hold faith as a shield, to quench all [the] flaming arrows of the evil one. And take the helmet of salvation and the sword of the Spirit, which is the word of God.
Ephesians 6:10-17

Leslie "Abraham" Grantham should be the title for the beautiful lady who inspired this prayer. But before we get ahead of ourselves, let's gather some of the background story.

My husband and I were neighbors with the Indianapolis Colts Center, Jeff Saturday. It was a true blessing getting to know Jeff and his family over the years and watch Jeff's career with quarterback Peyton Manning and the entire Colts team soar to exciting heights. One day, Karen Saturday called to invite us to join a couples' Bible Study in their home with a small group of people. We gladly accepted. Over the years, we grew very close to all in the group and loved every minute of our time together. It was a true blessing.

During our discussions, Jeff often fondly spoke of a special lady who tremendously impacted his faith. She was instrumental in praying for him throughout his life, and he gave her much of the credit for the man he had become. Although this special person was his mother, he had nicknamed her his personal Abraham.

Yes, he was making reference to the actual Biblical Abraham that makes his appearance in the very first book of the Bible, Genesis.

But when I asked Leslie why Jeff called her his Abraham, she honestly said she wasn't quite sure! Leslie is far too humble to place herself in Abraham's camp, so this part of the story I had to get from Jeff himself.

Jeff began referring to his mom as "his personal Abraham" sometime in his adulthood. It would never have occurred to him as a child, but looking back, he sees it clearly. He said assuredly, "her characteristics align themselves with Abraham." Abraham always placed his trust in God and sought to follow His will obediently, as does his mom, Leslie. Abraham also interceded for the sinful Sodom and Gomorrah, and this sweet lady also pleaded with the Lord for Jeff when he was in trouble and making bad choices. Abraham's faith in God was intense, and God credited it to him as righteousness; Leslie also has that kind of faith.

Jeff said it wasn't as much *that* his mom had faith but *how* she demonstrated her loyalty to her faith that made a lasting impact on him. Her sleep-deprived body rose every morning to prayer and Scripture. Her time with God, no matter how difficult it was to achieve, was a non-negotiable priority. Jeff knew no one else like her and certainly had no friends, relatives, or even mentors who mimicked this curious behavior.

As an adult, with children of his own, Jeff now looks back on those days and sees his mother's strength, will-power, wisdom, and fortitude. He understands that, like Abraham, her full and utter dependence on God protected their family through the storms. He knows now the power of those many prayers and believes he was raised by much more than a loving mom, for his heavenly Father was radiating from her soul and patiently penetrating, mending, and infusing hope into his brokenness.

A Tough Start for the Saturday Family

Leslie raised her children to love the Lord. That is, when she could be at home with them. As a single mother raising her two children alone, she was hard at work every day to pay the bills, keep a humble roof over their heads, and put just enough food in their tummies.

Leslie's husband left when Jeff was only a toddler, and his sister only four years old. Life was a true burden most days, and she often felt totally out of control. She yearned to have more time with her children and felt the heaviness of the cross she carried each day. Leslie didn't make a move without God, for she clearly understood that one wrong step could cost her dearly. Keeping herself in line and safe was one thing, but she needed heavenly bodyguards to watch over her children in the hours she could not be with them. She also needed them to guide and protect their precious hours together at home, allowing her to make the most out of every minute.

You could say Leslie entered into a special "heavenly contract" for the family she was to raise. Her request was bold yet humble as she asked for God's protection and guidance. Her end of the contract would be to raise her children in faith, take them to church, be an example to them through her own life, spend time in the classroom of prayer each day, consult with God always, and raise her children with the kind of love that encourages growth and demands responsibility.

God's part of the contract was to protect and guide her children and to assist Leslie in her words and actions toward them. She often prayed for the wisdom to see what she could not see and hear what she could not hear so that she could guide and keep her children on the right path. She told me with a chuckle, "Your children are not really yours. We are always in battle with another spiritual force for their souls."

Consequences were often leveraged in teaching her children: "if that, then this" was a common mantra for the Saturday household. Leslie said they all needed this reminder because "the Saturdays are known as strong-minded folk." Leslie knew from her own past that strong-minded people will always err doing it their own way. Consequences, she believed, were the stabilizers needed to keep the strong-willed humble and on track.

The Secret Place

Leslie took her role as a mother seriously, believing it was her job to give the gift from God back to Him for all of eternity. Her role was to do all she could to get her children to Heaven, and that task is not accomplished overnight or in a few weeks or months. It is a lifelong mission of discipline and faith that she still daily engages in, especially when she goes to her *Secret Place*.

Leslie's *Secret Place* can be wherever she is, but it is always in solitude. Somehow, she finds as little as a few minutes to more than an hour of time in prayer. It's just a simple conversation with the Creator to see what she needs to do and how to do it. She is adamant about always beginning with Scripture, so "God is the One who starts the conversation." Sometimes the answers to her questions are revealed before she says a word. Other times, Scripture is the calming influence that allows her mind to be open to what she needs to know and hear. She believes her relationship with God is like a marriage. "You can't continue to love, know, and honor a person if you never take the time to converse with them." She believes our ideas, challenges, and aspirations must be shared with our spouses in order to fight off the tendency to get bored and eventually drift apart. Leslie knows that heartfelt communication builds relationships, not only in people but also true for the God who created us in His very image and likeness.

The Father Figure and Dose of Hope (1st Relief)

God saw what was missing from the Saturday home and sent in some relief. What was missing was the virtue of HOPE. They had been given faith, and they knew about God, but hope is a necessary layer to fortify faith. Leslie warns that no matter how much faith you give your children, if hope is off the table, the devil will pounce. Because of her guilt over the divorce, working long hours away from the children, and the little money she was able to earn, Leslie never talked to the children about their futures. Her two smart, ambitious, and impressionable children were, indeed, searching for more, and Jeff was finding it in all the wrong places. The darkness began to roll in and was working overtime to tear down her family.

God sent Leslie an answer to prayer in the form of a loving man. This man had free will, however, and although he loved Leslie, he didn't know if he could handle two kids, especially the one who was heading down a bad path. A young Jeff Saturday was already spiraling out of control, and his "strong-minded" nature placed a wedge between them. Still, Doug Grantham, after some soul-searching, persisted in finding a way to make it work. He was a relief with many names— husband, father figure, supporter, leader, and a voice of wise counsel.

After the marriage of Leslie and Doug, they had to decide where to live. Doug's home was nicer and larger, but he humbly moved in with them because he didn't want to uproot the kids from their home. This was the first of many selfless decisions Doug would make to support and to love his new family.

Leslie wasn't able to save any money for the children's college, and so she never spoke about continuing education with them. She believes that when a wayward child sees that the life they have is the only one they will ever know, the "consequences" mantra she had preached for years quickly loses its steam. Consequences weren't the issue for Jeff. Instead, it became a dangerous game of trying not to get caught. Despite some of the bad choices, Doug still saw the children's potential and began a college savings program to instill the HOPE they needed for a better life.

Leslie and Doug often warned Jeff about his attitude toward authority. Jeff wanted to answer to no one but himself. "Everyone answers to someone," they would implore. "It is your choice. You either listen to and obey us knowing that our authority comes from loving you, or you will be put with someone who you will be forced to obey, but who doesn't love you." It was during these days of hardship that Leslie would pray fervently for her rebellious child, asking God to supply the precise words needed to make her point. She asked for the wisdom to walk away, resist the long speech, and let the perfect words flow into the ears of her son before he had a chance to shut her out.

The Ultimatum (2nd Relief)

Jeff was hanging with a rough crowd of kids who were all engaging in activities well beyond the normal teenage mischief. To hide his behavior, he secured a beeper that allowed him to move under cover of secrecy. He could communicate (through phone number or code) with his buddies in crime, keeping his movements hidden from his parents. He knew what he was doing was wrong, but still, the thrill was captivating to him. A defining moment for the Saturday family came when the high school coaches collectively decided it was time to call Jeff into their office for a chat. Leslie didn't know anything about the intervention. Jeff's older sister knew about some of the dangerous things Jeff was doing and blew the whistle on him.

The coaches confronted Jeff in his sophomore year of high school with a serious ultimatum, one he would never forget. It was time to turn his life around before it was too late. They knew of his dedication to all his sports (football, wrestling, baseball, soccer, and track) and they also knew, because they were also his teachers, of his academic potential. They leveraged his love for sports and told him that being a member of a team came with responsibilities. They clearly stated that his current behaviors were not in line with what they expected from their athletes and that if he didn't stop immediately, he had no place on their teams. They laced the ultimatum with encouragement and truths about the future he could experience if he took what they said to heart. They gave it to him straight, man-to-man, and left the decision to him.

Perhaps Jeff had been blind to his own potential, but the coaches' warning woke him up to a new perspective. Jeff clearly understood the candid talk; in fact, Jeff knew it before they even spoke it but didn't have the will power to make the necessary changes on his own. Now, with his coaches' backing and directive, he knew what needed to be done, and he wasted no time in removing himself from the rough crowd and putting a stop to all the dangerous behaviors.

This would be a turning point in Jeff's life, and his mother would recognize it as a huge gift. God untangled a knot that, without prayer, could have tied him to his past. The answer to our prayers can come through the intercession of others. "God never fails us, she admits. He opens eyes to the truth and removes the blinders Satan imposes on us so we can see." The strong message from the coaches, if coming instead from Leslie and Doug, would not have had the same impact. In fact, it could have pushed Jeff farther away. God chose well the team He wanted to deliver this important and timely lesson. The coaches were an integral part of God's game plan. This ultimatum, layered on top of the foundation of love his parents had already provided, inspired the young man to rethink his decisions. Filled with hope and a fresh perspective, a new Jeff emerged and eventually went on to play football for the University of North Carolina Tar Heels.

Jeff grew in maturity throughout his college years and continued making good choices. At this point in Jeff's mind, it wasn't a God force that inspired him; it was simply the enjoyment of doing the right thing and being rewarded for it. Jeff made a name for himself on the football field and was looking forward to a career in the NFL. On draft day, Jeff waited for his name to be called through the first round, and then the next, and the next...but Jeff's name was never called. The NFL closed the door on Jeff Saturday; however, God had a window in mind. Sometimes, in order to fit through the window God has planned for us, we need to get a bit smaller! That was the case for Jeff. God needed Jeff humble for this next role. Leslie's prayers for Jeff went beyond him just being a good person. Jeff could be much more, and God was in the process of establishing His mark on Jeff.

Jeff accepted a job and began his humble life off the field selling electrical supplies. God was working on him in the stillness of this season and preparing him for what He needed Jeff to do. Leslie was encouraging and supportive, reminding him that a call could come at any time. Jeff loved football, and she knew it could be a good thing for him, yet she was faithful to the God Who put that prayer on the back burner. God gave Jeff humility, and Leslie gave him hope. It was a winning combination.

The Career (3rd Relief)

It was late summer when a call came in from the Indianapolis Colts. They needed a center for Peyton Manning. This was the beginning of something beautiful— a song only God could write. This was a turning point, not only for his career but also for his soul. Jeff's humility never left him but rather became him, as if it seeped into his bones and transformed him into the Godly man he is. Jeff's growing faith would attract like-minded players, and they would become a strong force on and off the field. Athletes are given a unique stage to perform; what they do with it is up to them. Jeff's faith in the God who changed his life was always present—it was in the locker room, on the field, within his home, it reached out to a community and soon penetrated the hearts of all who followed him… and all of this happened because "someone" had taken the time to ask for God's help in prayer.

Leslie Grantham has memorized the Ephesians passage that opened this chapter. She calls upon these ancient words, written by St. Paul to the Ephesians, to guide, encourage, and defend her family.

A Prayer of Humble Gratitude for the Divine Desire to Know, Love and Serve You

Dear Almighty God,

Thank you for being my life-long and very dearest friend and for sending the Holy Spirit each day to fill my soul. As an only child, I depended on You like I would have a brother or sister. You were always there for me. Thank you for the family tree that instilled Your presence within me and prayed for me. I have felt the sincerity and power of their prayers throughout my life.

I thank you for answering my prayers, even those I have yet to utter. Sometimes You have spared me the difficult stuff, and sometimes You have laid it upon my cross. With Your graces of strength and perseverance, I am able to follow You anywhere You choose to take me. The more I know You, the more I need You in my life, and for that Divine desire, I am grateful.

Praying Your Child Through Anything

You use my strong-minded and perceptive nature to identify evil strongholds within my family so I can pray to You about them. The strongholds are frightening at times and leave me desperate for Your guidance. Sometimes I see our strong-willed family forge roads of their own, stretching their independence to places of danger. Your love and Your mercy, however, envelope this family, and it is those special graces that serve as the common thread weaving us together. No family is perfect, but we do have Your perfect love, and with it, we will continue to love each other.

I ask, as always, that You temper my words and soften my actions so that all advice, counsel, concern, and judgment come from a place of respect and love. At times, I just want to blurt out the offense, like a ref blowing a whistle on the field. Other times, I want to immediately fix the situation without thinking through the inherent consequences. Adjust my timing to be Your holy timing and guide me to act according to Your Almighty will, not mine. Help me to stand up for what I know to be right and just, but with the patience You desire me to exercise.

You have raised Jeff to be a patriarch for our family. His sons and daughter are following in his footsteps, and I pray for them to be leaders like their dad and mom are today. We look up to Jeff because he is close to You. He has much on his shoulders, but You raised a strong and humble man to fight these battles and to lead this family closer to You. I pray for all leaders, but especially for the ones You place in the spotlight. They can opt for the easy path, or they can choose YOUR way of truth and light. It is not easy. It is not always safe. It goes against the mainstream. It can seem lonely. But it is the only way to eternal peace and joy. Amen.

This prayer was inspired by Leslie Grantham.

The bio of Leslie's son, Jeff Saturday: Jeff Saturday is a Super Bowl XLI champion, AFC champion in Super Bowl XLIV, and six-time Pro Bowl Center who played thirteen years for the Indianapolis Colts (1999-2011) with quarterback Peyton Manning. Together, Saturday and Manning started an NFL record 172 games as a center-quarterback duo. Jeff also played one year with the Green Bay Packers (2012) and ended his career with a one-day contract, retiring as an Indianapolis Colt.

While a player for the Colts, Saturday was a member of the Executive Committee of the National Football League Players' Association. During the 2011 NFL lockout, when unresolved issues brought both sides to the bargaining table, it was the highly respected Jeff Saturday who was instrumental in negotiating the long-term Collective Bargaining Agreement that ended the lockout.

Jeff joined ESPN in 2013 and appears on *NFL Live* and *SportsCenter* as well as contributes to other ESPN platforms. He remains an active part of his community, whether it be coaching a high school football team or filling a need for a charitable cause. Some of his endeavors include: Kid's Voice of Indiana, People' Burn Foundation of Indiana, Riley Hospital for Children, and Susan G. Komen for the Cure.

Prayer Prompt

God uses His holy ones to complete His work on Earth. He can choose to send a message of hope through a multitude of souls to the one in need. We must be ready to act when needed and also to accept help when we are moved to the sidelines. Remember, God is in control.

Meditation Prayer For Parents
Whose Lost Child Needs a Dose of Hope

Dear God,

I fear for my lost child and for the evil strongholds placed on [him/her]. [name] thinks [he/she] is choosing freedom but has no idea of the tremendous debt associated with an evil master. Help me find my child's unique "hope" that will trigger the turnabout. Reach through the darkness to send relief to our family. Open [name] eyes to the shackles of lies [he/she] has been chained to and the sinful behaviors that bind [him/her] in shame. Remind [name] of the bottomless mercy that is [his/hers] for the asking and the glorious freedom that comes with sincere repentance.

I know [name] heart is good and that [he/she] knows right from wrong, but evil has a way of tainting the world and sugar coating the most horrific acts. You have faithful warriors who come in contact with my [son/daughter] on a daily basis. Please mobilize all Your faithful warriors in [his/her] path and bless them with the courage to speak up, the humility to lead by example, and the empathy to encourage a wayward soul.

Help me understand the simplicity of a parent's true love and the far-reaching corners it can penetrate when it has heavenly wings carrying it. Help me to be a model of faith and a beacon of hope for my family and for others around me. Protect us from the darkness of evil and break any stronghold it has placed over us. For You, dear heavenly Father, are the only Master we desire to serve and the only freedom we hope for. Amen.

Praying Your Child Through Anything
...Even the Walk Home to be With God

"We have been promised something we do not yet possess. It is good for us to persevere in longing until we receive what was promised, and yearning is over."
Saint Augustine

I walked into a room to interview two mothers who had both walked their young children home to be with God. Pam Frenzel and Cyndi McGinnis each had their own story to tell, yet the intertwining of the stories is something to behold. The two mothers were very close; they were sisters. Their alliance to one another reached a deeper level than most siblings could ever imagine. What you might not fully understand – yet was apparent during our talk – were the small, yet profound, blessings that God sends to accompany the sadness.

One sister finished the thought of the other while the other stirred a sweet memory that caused them both to blush. Tender smiles often spanned across their faces. I watched, amazed, as the harmony played out, learning they shared something both devastating yet spectacular and sorrowful yet ultimately exultant. It is difficult to imagine all these emotions coming from one conversation, but God works like that.

Pam lost her son Tyler to Leukemia, and Cyndi's daughter Maggie would succumb to a rare disease called Ewing's Sarcoma. Cancer would attack Pam's son first, while Cyndi would play the supporting role. Eight years later, Cyndi's daughter would fight the cancer battle, leaving Pam to support her sister. It is difficult to imagine what each sister went through, as they not only lost a child, they also lost their nephew or niece. They interacted so reverently and thoughtfully toward each other and told me that when they share stories of Tyler and Maggie, they stand on holy ground. I felt it. It surrounded us.

Both mothers agreed that the most overwhelming feeling each of them experienced was the peace they received in their total surrender to God. Ultimately, it was the only way they could withstand the pain, knowing there was nothing more they could do for their children. The days of kissing away the hurt of a cut or scrape were gone. This was bigger than motherhood, bigger than fatherhood, bigger than nurses, doctors, and surgeons. This was not to be remedied on earth; instead, it was in God's loving hands, with His timing, and in His way.

"It's a club you never want to be in," said Pam and Cyndi. "That is, until you find out who the president of the club is!" With humble smiles and confident voices, they announced her name. "It is Mary, the Mother of Jesus, who sweetens our crosses and comforts our pains. She understands, she truly understands."

Pam and Her Son Tyler

Tyler Christian Frenzel was diagnosed with Leukemia in 2002 and fought an uphill battle for two painful and exhausting years, with his personal motto of: *No Limits, Fight Hard, Never Give Up!* Accomplishing all God had planned for Tyler's short time on earth, the nine-year-old boy was taken home on December 11, 2004.

Pam explained that it is unbearable to see your child suffer such an agonizing and brutal death. Tyler consumed every thought she had and every prayer she could muster. For many months she, along with hundreds of friends and family, prayed for a total healing miracle. She pleaded with God and even tried to negotiate terms so Tyler could receive the miracle *she* wanted him to be granted. Pam begged for mercy and glorified God with adoring confidence, for she knew of His almighty power, Omnipotence, and absolute ability to command the impossible. If He had chosen to answer her plea, Tyler would have become pain-free, smiling, and strong.

One day, in prayer, God turned Pam's heart inside out. He spoke to her soul in a way He had never done before, or perhaps, she wonders, if she was finally desperate enough to simply listen. God's answer was bold, touching, and poignant. "Tyler is your miracle, dear child. Don't miss it!"

Tyler is the miracle? The words took a few minutes to register. Could it be that God had already answered her prayers, and the miracle she needed was already here? She knew the voice was real, for along with it came such peace and confirmation. Pam opened her heart to understand His words and looked at Tyler through the eyes of God. Indeed, Tyler *was* the miracle, and he demonstrated it to the community around him with his unwavering faith and his courage in suffering day after day. Tyler's mom, filled with intense love for her son, had nearly missed the beautiful package sitting beside her because it wasn't the miracle she had prayed, begged, and pleaded for. Pam realized God had given her much more than she asked for. In that moment, she learned that God cannot be outdone in His generosity. Pam embraced and surrendered *her* miracle to the miracle God had just graciously revealed to her.

Once again, God spoke into the soul of Pam for confirmation and resolve. She heard these words, "He is not yours to keep." This tender yet somber message helped Pam see her children in an entirely new light and allowed her to more easily relinquish parental control to Tyler's Creator. God does not take children from us; He calls them back to Himself and the eternal home He has prepared for each of them. Pam said she then realized, "They are not mine, but children of God."

With fresh eyes and a new perspective, she steeped in the glory of her son like never before. She soaked up his words like a sponge and filled her eyes with his gestures and movements. She engaged in his battle and allowed her motherly strength to pour out to him. Tyler had the kind of faith that moves mountains, and through this journey, Tyler and Pam became even closer, and she could feel a heavenly presence whenever she was near him. Jesus and Mary guided them through this time; as it was their story, of a sorrowful mother and dying son, that most affected and comforted them as they prayed.

Tyler's cross was heavy with pain, yet he could not stop talking about how close he felt to God. Pam's cross was painful in a different way, for like the Blessed Mother, her heart was pierced at the suffering of her son. Tyler and Pam trusted in the intercession of Jesus and Mary and followed their example of how to pick up their cross each day with hope.

Before Tyler died, he told Pam he often prayed for her. She was the one he was most worried about and wondered how she would cope after he was gone. He never worried about himself, but instead for the family that would survive his passing, being left with sorrow, distress, and many unanswered questions.

Those days following Tyler's death were a blur as Pam began to pull herself out of the rubble left by the two-year storm called Leukemia. It had taken its toll and left their family bruised, battered, and broken. She remembers going through the motions, unaware of her surroundings. Each member of the family felt Tyler's loss in their own way. It was one household with many compartments of sorrow. God wrapped the entire family in His love, allowing time to lessen the pain of loss before gently nudging them to open their eyes to the new world around them. Focused on the beauty still left in their home, they found the courage to wake, to trust, and to bond once again. It was as if God gathered the tattered threads of each family member and, using their many prayers and love for each other, wove for them a new family tapestry.

A priest who was mentoring Pam through her deep sorrow gave her this advice: "The loneliness will become your friend. In the loneliness, you will feel your child most present, and the presence of Jesus will surround you." Pam said she was grateful for this prophetic insight and looks at loneliness with spiritual eyes and is grateful for the comfort it has brought her through the different seasons of grief. When things begin to spiral down, it is this thankful place she seeks in the solitude of her soul. If only for a short time, she can embrace the emptiness, allowing the graces of God to fill her with fond memories, joy, and peace.

Cyndi and Her Daughter Maggie

Magdalena "Maggie" Rose Elder was diagnosed on June 11, 2011 with an aggressive stage four cancer called Ewing's Sarcoma, which had begun with a pelvic tumor within her eleven-year-old body. On

February 22, 2012 (just eight brief months later) she, too, like her cousin Tyler was called to heaven.

Cyndi's wound was more fragile than Pam's when we sat down to talk. When Maggie was diagnosed with cancer, it had been only five and a half years since Tyler's passing. I still cannot imagine burying both a child and a niece or nephew in such a short period of time. The wounds of Tyler's battle had just begun to heal when another sword of cancer would cut through their family again, opening up old wounds and creating new ones. The pain and shock are hard to comprehend. Perhaps it was the bond of sisterhood, strengthened by Tyler's journey, that they would use to comfort each other and allow God to take control. I'm not sure what it was, but it was present, and it was powerful hearing about the path they forged together.

Maggie was a homebody of sorts and Cyndi's little shadow. She was up for having fun over at a friend's house but would always choose to return to her home rather than spending the night. Cyndi never minded because she, herself, cherished their solitude and private lives. Mother and daughter flew under the social radar and were happiest outside the limelight. But with the onset of the illness, Maggie was in the spotlight. Their once private sanctuary was now revealed for all to see. Word spread quickly, and people began to take notice when an eleven-year-old girl is given only two months to live. Maggie was on prayer lists all over the country. Their lives changed so dramatically and were in such stark contrast to the peaceful world they left behind.

Ewing's Sarcoma is a rare cancer with, unfortunately, no known cure. Maggie's condition, therefore, raised attention among numerous medical teams. Trying to extend the two months originally given her to live, they attempted many therapies to slow or reverse the spread of cancer throughout her young body. Maggie endured seemingly endless days of exams, blood tests, and promising procedures. Privacy was non-existent, and Cyndi's heart broke for her modest and innocent child, whose failing body was constantly on display. Maggie's days were filled with pain as she was tortured and sickened from the cancer, and then again from the one hopeful cure that remained useless within her body.

Cyndi shared a memory with me that left a mark on my heart. Maggie's eleven years of age had not given her much experience with death and dying. She had lots of questions about the endless doctor visits, and she wanted to know what was going to happen to her. Cyndi reached deep in her heart to explain to her little Velcro buddy that she would be going somewhere that Cyndi was unable to follow. She wondered how she could possibly prepare Maggie for an eternal journey that existed far away from the only home she had ever known. Through prayer, Cyndi found the perfect place to lovingly map out the future that awaited Maggie. In Eucharistic adoration,* Cyndi sat with Maggie's head resting in her lap. "It's so peaceful here," Maggie would tell her mom over and over again. It became the best place for Cyndi to actually show her daughter what Heaven was like and to reassure her of the genuine peace she would find through trusting Jesus.

For every poke and procedure Maggie endured, the hospital gave a reward bead. Cyndi and Maggie took those beads, fastened them together into a beautiful rosary, and hung it from Maggie's IV pole that never left her side. As the days grew darker, Cyndi's faith grew stronger, and she knew our Blessed Mother would be there for her daughter when she was no longer able. All Cyndi had to do was shift Maggie from her own earthly arms into the heavenly arms of our Blessed Mother. This image brought Cyndi incredible comfort, and she trusted that Mary would watch over, hold, and comfort her daughter in Heaven. Our Blessed Mother Mary knew what to do, for she once swaddled Jesus as a baby, cared for him as a child, and then held him as he was lowered from the cross. With kindred spirits, they would be united in motherhood, through the sweet joys of loving and the bitter sorrows of loss.

Knowing that someday they would be reunited in Heaven, Cyndi's and Maggie's faith allowed hope to seep in and melt the fears away. God's amazing grace and abundant love would forever hold them together.

Cyndi wrote to me after our interview to clarify some of the things we discussed. Her words are so heartfelt and sincere, that I believe others will find comfort and hope in her recounting of the days leading up to the loss of her sweet daughter.

> "The most difficult part for me is that Jesus was in our midst in a tangible way, as if I had to say "excuse me" to step around him in the kitchen or family room while serving Maggie. This is the Holy Ground. God was in our home with Maggie throughout the journey (we experienced this with Tyler also). Other people felt it when entering our homes. God comes for the children. He comes to strengthen and comfort the parents and family. When Maggie was called home, that tangible presence of Jesus went with her. I wept for the absence of Maggie. I wept for the absence of my Father God. How could you leave me now?! The valley of the shadow of death is a place of abandonment, but my faith never wavered. I had to walk blindly and trust His promises. This is the ultimate test of one's faith."

Maggie once feared death but taught Cyndi to always trust God. Maggie said, "Faith can CRUSH fear," and for both of them, it did exactly that. Great things have sprouted because of Maggie's faith, and others are being helped through the "Miracles from Maggie" organization.

A Prayer for Tyler

Dear Father in Heaven,

Tyler and I followed carefully each footprint you left for us, and we clung to the Almighty voice that guided us through our darkest days. Never did we stray from our trusted Shepherd, and our strides became uniform and synchronized with the One who knew well the path ahead. Looking back, I now see clearly the treacherous road we traveled and the many pitfalls you saved us from. Thank you for Your tender companionship and steadfast guidance.

I come to you today in thanksgiving for the nine years you allowed Tyler to be part of our earthly family. Our home now extends into heaven, where pain no longer consumes his body and where his comfort comes from you.

Slowly You mended me; stitch-by-stitch You so carefully worked. You sent people into my life who filled the gaps within my soul, and the threads, once scattered, began pulling together. If I could imagine my heart, it would be a patchwork of fragments sewn back together with the threads of Your love. So strong is my heart now, for Your divine hands wove it back together. Your almighty and divine fingerprints will remain within me forever.

Don't ever let me stray from you. Don't ever let me know a day I do not praise you for the gifts that surround me. Don't let me miss the miracles, dear Lord, as you allow me to notice and experience your many blessings still active in my life.

Please give Tyler a big hug from me and tell him his prayers are working. I am going to make it! I remain Yours and will forever follow Your lead, Amen.

This prayer was inspired by the interview with
Pam Frenzel, mother of Tyler.

***

Prayers for Maggie

You will find two prayers attributed to Maggie, a prayer at the beginning of the climb and a prayer to move forward. *A Prayer to Begin the Journey* was written by her mother, Cyndi McGinnis, the same week thirteen-year-old Maggie was diagnosed with Ewing's Sarcoma and given only two months to live. The post of this prayer entered later into the pages of Maggie's Caring Bridge, is a reminder to each of us of the extreme faith it takes to even approach the mountain that has been set before us. She titled this prayer, *A Mother's Plea*.

A Prayer to Begin the Journey: *A Mother's Plea*

Dear Heavenly Father,

You are bigger than cancer. If it is your will, you will heal Maggie, and it will be considered a miracle—one of your finest...

Please heal Maggie, Lord. I beg you. I want more time with her here. I cannot imagine life without her—my Velcro buddy...my shadow... my mirror... and yet, she never really was my daughter. She is your child. And I was given the incredible privilege of being her earthly mother.

If it is your will to call her Home after such a short time here on Earth, then PLEASE, I desperately need your grace and strength to accept your will and walk my daughter home to you, her heavenly Father. Thank you for honoring me with the most precious gift of being Maggie's mom. In Jesus' name, Amen.

A Prayer to Move Forward

It has been three years since I last held Maggie, and my heart still bleeds tears of mourning. My most tender feelings spill out onto canvas, and the brush becomes my therapy. For years I have held tightly to the cross of her death, and You, like a trusted friend, have sat with me while I was mourning. You are calling me to a new life, and I am learning to live without Maggie through Your grace, yet I still find myself immersed in the sorrow that envelopes me. I try to make sense of how this pain can bring You glory and why it has lasted so long within my soul. I trust in Your plan and believe You make all things new.

Please know, even in the sorrow, I am most grateful for what You have given me. You knew how special Maggie would be to this world and the impact she would make on so many souls. She was a beacon of hope to those who knew and loved her. Especially the hospital staff, who spent months patiently caring for her frail and failing body, were gifted with the immense joy found within her vibrant soul.

How long would Maggie have had to spend on Earth for her to demonstrate Your love? Oh, Gracious Lord, spending even one day with Maggie delivers a lifetime of smiles. You granted many days to me—even years, before you requested her return. For that, I am forever grateful. I am honored You gave me the gift of Maggie's life to treasure. It was an honor to serve such a sweet and caring soul. You chose to work this spectacular miracle of life through me, and I am grateful for each day I had with Maggie, my teacher in life, who taught me both how to live and how to die.

Where, I wonder, are we going with this new cross you have given me? Lead me, dear Lord. Allow me to share my experience if it will comfort others. Please, God, help me to carry my cross with strength and grace in a way that draws others closer to you. With Your divine mercy, I can do all things through You, who strengthens me. Amen

---

This prayer was inspired by the interview with
Cyndi McGinnis, Maggie's mom.

Eucharistic Adoration - In Roman Catholic Church tradition, Adoration is the practice of adoring or venerating Jesus (body, blood, soul, and divinity) through the Holy Eucharist. The Holy Eucharist is the communion host that has been consecrated by a priest during Mass, which has turned the common bread and wine into the true body and blood of our Lord, Jesus Christ. Once consecrated, this bread and wine become spiritual food and are no longer regarded as mere bread and mere wine. Since this transubstantiation has occurred by the power of God through his vessel, the priest, it shall be revered and adored. During Adoration, the consecrated host is elevated and held within an open or transparent receptacle called a monstrance, so that the faithful can venerate and visit Jesus in a most intimate way. Adoration is offered in Roman Catholic churches across the country at specific times during the year. Many churches offer perpetual Adoration (24 hours a day and seven days a week without break). One interesting note: Once the consecrated host is exposed (not contained within the tabernacle but is exposed within a monstrance), it may not be left alone and requires a person to be present at all times. For complete coverage, adorers will sign up for a block of time in which they take responsibility to be present with Jesus.

Prayer Prompt

Meditate on the Seven Sorrows of Mary*

Personally, I have found much wisdom and healing from this devotion. My first book, The Seven Sorrows Bible Study for Catholics, what we can learn from Our Mother of Sorrows, was the inspirational result of many hours in prayer, meditation, and contemplation as I studied Jesus' sorrow-filled events from the eyes of His Mother, Mary.

Allow the Blessed Mother's seven sorrows to speak to you during your grief. She has been where you are now. Mary was at the foot of the Cross of Christ, and she will bring you there to lovingly embrace you, hold you, and teach you. It is true that we meet the best people at the foot of the cross. This Gentle Woman will gladly introduce you to her friends, who all gather there to be closer to her Son. Mary invites you to unburden your heart by sharing your sufferings and grief with her. Allow the softness of Mary to lead you to the powerful arms of her Son, Jesus, who longs to help you. He is waiting. Imagine your meeting. What will you say?

Meditation Prayer for Those Parents Who Have Lost a Child

Dear Lord God,

I love You. I want You. I need You. My heart yearns for Your embrace as I find it so difficult to live a life without [name]. A part of my heart went with [him/her] when You called [him/her] home to be with You. I ponder all of [his/her] earthly milestones, had [he/she] remained here with me. I try to imagine the glory of heaven and the joy that [name] is now experiencing within Your Eternal Kingdom. I yearn for the special day I, too, will be called to join You, but I know Your work is not complete within my soul. Help me make the most of every day and honor the memory of [name]. I know You are close to [him/her] so I want to be close to You. Let Your will work through me until we can all be together again. Thank You, dear Father, for Your thoughtfulness in how You choose to comfort me, and please know that I am truly overjoyed with immense gratitude for the blessing You assigned me when You created [name] to be my beloved [son/daughter]. Amen.

- The Seven Sorrows of Mary— Luke's Gospel (2: 33-35) tells of when Joseph and Mary took their baby Jesus up to the temple for the Presentation. Simeon, the profit, greets them and offers them some startling insight about their precious child. One of the things he says to Mary is that a sword will pierce her so that the thoughts of many hearts may be revealed. He is speaking in reference to how the will of God shall be manifested through Jesus and the sorrow it will carry. Paintings often depict Mary with seven swords piercing her heart, and these images are widely known as the Seven Sorrows of Mary. The sorrows are as follows:

    1. The Prophesy of Simeon (Luke 2:25-35)
    2. The Massacre of the Innocent (Matthew 2:13-18)
    3. The Loss of the Child Jesus for Three Days (Luke 2:41-52)
    4. The Meeting of Jesus and Mary on the Way of the Cross (Luke 23:26-32)
    5. The Crucifixion (John 19:16-30)
    6. Taking Jesus Down from the Cross (Mark 15: 42-47)
    7. The Burial of Jesus (John 19: 39-42)

    Meditating on Jesus' mother's sorrows has aided many in their own struggles, especially when a loved one is the one suffering. Jesus suffered greatly for our salvation and Mary, his mother, was front and center for all of it. Her face, on the way of the cross, can also represent our own faces as we look upon him who suffers and allow him to take refuge in a Mother's softness and the most tender of all loves known to man.

Afterword

Praying Your Child Through Anything
...Even an Addiction to Heroin

This is one chapter I did not have to interview another parent about because I was blessed to have lived it myself. You might wonder why a parent would ever use the word blessed when talking about heroin addiction, but I can explain. God boomeranged my intense prayers for my daughter right back onto me and the need for a cleansing in my own life. The journey through addiction brought me such peace; a peace I didn't even realize I was lacking. Moreover, it most likely was the hidden inspiration God used to place the writing of this book upon my heart. I planned only to interview other parents, capturing their stories of faith, and had not thought to contribute my own story. These courageous parents spilled their hearts out so that you, the reader, might find solace in their trials. Perhaps, I thought, my story might serve you as well.

The angle of this afterword differs slightly from the others' chapters, as I believe my encounter with addiction was more than a profound opportunity to pray for my child; it was a wake-up call from God regarding my own life. My journey into parenthood was used to transform, soften, and expand my heart. I assume most parents, if they looked deep enough, would also see how God changed them as He sharpened and clarified their many gifts as their children grew. Through my daughter, who was addicted to heroin, I painfully discovered God's treasure chest of humility. Calloused from years of clinging to the false security of pride, God coaxed me to let go and trust Him.

My Rough Edges

I was an above-average student in a medium-sized high school in a small mid-western town. If high schools have three tiers of students, with the popular kids at the top, I was somewhere in the second tier with most of the class. I knew several of the popular kids and occasionally would hang out with them except when they were drinking or partying. I was never invited to anyone's home for such a bash, and people would get pretty quiet if I happened upon a conversation about a party they went to or one they were planning.

As far as the third tier goes, they were the hard-core partiers, most likely drinking alcohol before or during school and using, buying, and selling drugs. I had no use for them and would do everything I could to avoid contact. I didn't learn their names, even if they were in my homeroom, and I certainly didn't sit by them at lunch. I wondered why they made such bad choices, bringing trouble and grief upon themselves. I also made the broad assumption that they must not have a caring family, for if they did, they certainly wouldn't be drawn to drugs. I considered them to be on the losing side of life, and I judged them accordingly.

God Sent a Blessing

Flash-forward twelve years, when my husband, Bill, and I were holding in our arms the sweetest baby we could have imagined. We drove to the attorney's office as a couple and left as a family. As the adoption papers were being drawn up, we began planning all the things we could now do with our new daughter. I loved Sarah instantly, and her smile was contagious. A happy baby 99.9% of the time, I swore to myself that if I ever damaged this precious spirit, I would never forgive myself.

Throughout elementary school, Sarah remained joyful, funny and full of life. She had many girl and boy friends, worked hard in school, participated in several sports, and enjoyed many activities. It was in middle school that Bill and I began to notice her consistent withdrawal. It seemed as if an avalanche of gremlins hit her all at once. The dynamics at school changed with the onset of unhealthy competition and cliques. She had three years in a row where teachers, for different and legitimate reasons, took months off of teaching during the school year. Attending a private Catholic school with three classrooms per grade, most of the students did not hit the trifecta of lost teachers, as Sarah did. This inconsistency in learning methods, brought on by a slew of substitute teachers, added to her anxiety, and her academics greatly suffered. We discovered, through numerous talks, input from her teachers, and our own observations, that she was fighting something that none of us knew how to fix, so we got help. The diagnosis was ADHD (Attention Deficit Disorder), and the solution was a series of controlled-substance medications, which we later discovered would be her gateway to hard-core drug use.

During her senior year in high school, she lied to us about even the smallest things, broke curfew, lost most of her good friends, hid her whereabouts, drank alcohol on her way to school, smoked cigarettes, and desired a secret life. She was confrontational, paranoid, and her behaviors were completely out of control. She knew the words that would hurt us the most and used them to push us away; she wished we had never adopted her, and she hated us being her parents.

What was especially difficult is that our family lost the immense joy Sarah had always showered upon us. We all mourned that void along with having to deal with the new and emerging Sarah, filled with anger, bitterness, and resentment. It caused great strife for us as her parents and especially with her sister, Moira, just one year younger than she. Sarah and Moira were best friends for as long as they could remember, but this metamorphosis created a dangerous, and at times seemed to be an irrevocable, chasm between them.

When Sarah wasn't home, we scoured her bedroom for the drugs we suspected she was on. Thinking she might have stashed something away for later, we searched for the answer. She admits now that she was sneaky at hiding things, using a clothes pocket or the most obscure objects to hide her drugs. Later, after she knew she needed help, she allowed us to confiscate a spoon, empty tin foil wrappers, and a lighter.

Our sweet daughter was an addict. Not just with any drug, but she had worked her way up to a big one named heroin. It brought us to our knees. Waking with a start in the middle of the night, my husband and I would go to her bedroom. Sometimes our fears would subside as we saw her asleep in her bed, but several nights she was nowhere to be found. Crawling out a bedroom window, she would go to find what her body relentlessly craved. If buying it from a car window in a seedy part of town wasn't dangerous enough, we also knew the extreme chances she took with every needle she used, fearful it would cause an unexpected overdose.

Sarah was admitted twice into inpatient drug rehabilitation centers and also lived a few months in a safe home. Our hearts crumbled into pieces each time we dropped Sarah off at a facility that we hoped would keep her safe for at least a while. She, her therapists, and doctors would talk it out. They would teach her the tools necessary to combat the disease and arm her with the newest programs to help her stay sober. We prayed it would be enough to strengthen her resolve against her addiction. Several of the addicts her age, who we met in the treatment centers, did not make it. Sarah frequently learned via social media that one by one, they had succumbed to an overdose. Even many of the strongest had been robbed of their adult life before it even began.

Before and between the times in rehab, life could get downright ugly living with an addict. My husband and I took turns wanting to throw her out of the house, thanking God in hindsight that His Almighty wisdom never let both of us desire it at the same time. One of us always calmed down the other and brought new perspective back into the discussion. I hate to think how a rash decision could have changed the trajectory of Sarah's life.

Smoothing Out the Rough Edges, God's Way

It was on one particular night that God spoke to me. Sarah was going through heroin withdrawal, so I was sleeping with her to keep watch and to help her through it. During heroin withdrawal, a body craves the drug so viciously that it sends torrents of tremors, or seizure-like episodes, throughout the legs, torso, and neck. They are often very severe and painful because of the uncontrollable and sporadic jerking movement made when the body desires a fix. To work through it takes incredible resilience, and many lack the willpower, eventually giving in to the temptation. When one of her episodes would commence, she would wake me up and ask me to wrap my arms around her petite frame and hold her as tightly as I could. This helped calm the convulsions she was experiencing several times during the night.

I prayed like never before and asked God to spare this child, giving me the strength to help her through another night. I literally had nothing more to give, but I knew God still had everything. Surrendering my soul to the Creator, I allowed Him complete control over me. Sarah couldn't see me but, as I held her, I wept huge tears onto the pillow. I was clinging on for dear life to the daughter I didn't want to lose...to the horrible addiction, the joy-robber, and the child-stealer.

In this torment of tears, God immediately flashed me back to my high school years, where my fears, pride, and arrogance cast a shadow over the same kind of people I was now begging for Him to spare. He showed me the flaw in my judgment, and He distinctly pointed to the antipathy I had allowed to breed within my soul. Many times, throughout Sarah's battle, I wondered if even one engaging or kind soul from middle school or high school could have possibly helped make a difference in Sarah's life, keeping her from wanting to try the hardcore drugs. Had I missed an opportunity to be God's light to a classmate who needed me?

I was heartbroken and ashamed for the missed opportunities to prevent this nightmare of addiction for another family. Perhaps I should have given them a smile at school or learned their name and offered a personal hello as we passed in the hallway. God placed me at that school during those years and with His people for a reason. Whether or not I could have made a difference, I now will never know because I didn't even try.

In order to correct my grave error of judgment in my youth, He formed and sent to Earth, a sweet baby girl, and allowed me to love her unconditionally. He softened my heart and taught me a better way to love through parenting. God knew that my many flaws and lack of willingness to understand were barring me from His Almighty plan within my life. The rough edges needed smoothing, and I needed to depend on God for everything. Pride limits my ability to love, so He pushed me beyond my limits. I could either remain in the bondage of my will, my way, my pride, or open my heart to the freedom humility brings as I walk in His will, His way, and His love.

As I held my daughter that night, the tears were for me, not her, as I finally broke. The hardness in my heart melted away, and I opened up my soul to a more forgiving and accepting life. *I loved an addict?* The magnitude of it had not fully penetrated my soul until that night. All those years of safeguarding my heart with superficial walls of pride, fear, and arrogance came tumbling down. I finally understood. Yes, indeed, I loved an addict. I was fearlessly holding tightly to an addict going through severe withdrawal. I kissed the hair of an addict and wiped her sweating face. I wanted to help Sarah survive another day and find the answers she was desperately searching for. And, I wanted to protect her from the judgment she would receive just for being an addict. In essence, I wanted to protect her from all the past versions of myself that failed to show love and mercy to an addict. The very behavior I had judged for most of my life became the sweet balm God used to heal my soul.

Our prayers were answered, and our daughter beat the odds and has completely turned her life around. Sarah has blessed us with a wonderful grandson, and we are crazy in love with him. He has his mom's great sense of humor! What a multitude of blessings we have been given. What a journey my soul has taken with God at the helm.

The Lesson

The up-close and intimate relationship with heroin addiction drastically changed my heart and my life. If I did not have my faith, I am confident I could not have made it through. Since then, I have rewritten the old saying, *God will never give you more than you can handle.* In looking back, I am quite certain He did indeed give me more than I could handle. God knows my finite limitations, and He also knows His own to be infinitely limitless. He is Almighty! When I was approaching my limit, God knew I would lean deeper into Him for support. When I hit my limit, God knew I would stop the car and ask Him for directions. And when my limit overflowed, He knew I would finally scoot over, give Him the wheel, and ask Him to take over. I now believe, with all my heart, that the saying should read like this: *God will never give you more than **He** can handle **through** you.* It was God who carried me, comforted me, and strengthened me. I am so weak on my own, but when He works through me, I am unstoppable. I was empowered to turn everything over to God so

He could work through me to help my daughter. It was the single most important lesson I have ever learned.

Prayer Prompt

Please reflect on how God is using your parenthood to build up His kingdom. The more we desire to understand His ways, the more He will share with us. God is using my child to:

- *sharpen and utilize my many talents and gifts*
- *challenge me to surrender a former misconception*
- *teach me a virtue, like patience or humility*
- *help me understand the beauty of a child-like faith*
- *allow wisdom to flow from one generation to the next throughout my family*
- *soften my heart and sanctify my soul*
- *bring me closer to Him, so He can strengthen me*
- *entice me to pray more frequently out of love for my child*
- *Add your own _____*

My Closing Prayer to You

The Master has a proposal to get you to eternity with Him. You are a part of His Almighty and Divine plan, as were the generations that preceded you and the ones that will follow. Prayer is how each of us communicates with our Creator to better understand the important role he has assigned to us.

Prayer can seem ambiguous at times, as we wonder just how heaven processes our many requests. There are no bandwidth constraints as each sentiment flows freely and expeditiously to God's ear. God never forgets a single prayer we utter. Because of His omnipotent and omnipresent nature, our prayers become timeless in the hands of God. He can choose to use our prayers whenever and as frequently as He desires. Our prayers can flow backwards in time to aid someone who passed before we were born, forward to fortify a person we may never know, or in the present to soothe a weary soul. In essence, a prayer we say today may be used to strengthen a great-great grandchild we will never share time on Earth with. We can, and should, pray for our entire family tree – past, present, and future.

God doesn't send us a bill for services rendered, and He certainly doesn't penalize us for late gestures of gratitude. His generosity overflows, and His patience toward each of us is overwhelmingly courteous. He loves us; I mean, He truly loves us in a way we cannot comprehend.

We never know who our prayers will bless and how much strength they will gather from the Holy Spirit as they approach heaven and come back again from God as graces. We do know that God hears every single prayer, even the ones that were only a brief thought. Keep praying your child through anything… He is listening!

God bless,
Beth Leonard

About the Author

Beth Leonard is a cradle Catholic who is inspired by meditation and prayer to follow God's lead wherever it may take her. She enjoys the many doors God has opened for her across the country and world through her books. She believes people are hungry to experience His Divine and Almighty Power, but lack the invitation and confidence to enter into that spiritual world. Beth writes to help people satisfy their craving for a true connection to God. She says, "We all know we are hungry for something; we just don't know whether to satisfy that need by cracking open the fridge or the Bible!"

Beth believes that God has a plan for every soul on Earth and it is our job to collaborate with him through prayer and study to uncover our unique path forward. Allowing God to work through her has been the best decision she has ever made.

Her works, to date, include writing three books, speaking to religious groups and guiding spiritual retreats. She loves immersing herself in Holy Scripture and learning about the early Church Fathers, Saints and Doctors of the Church. Beth lives with her husband, Bill, in Carmel, Indiana and they are parishioners of Immaculate Heart of Mary Parish.

For more information, visit Beth on her website BethLeonardBooks.com

Beth's other books… that were written to help you on that journey:

The Seven Sorrows Bible Study for Catholics, what we can learn from our Mother of Sorrows

Blood of the Lamb Catholic Bible Study, shed seven times to save us.

www.ingramcontent.com/pod-product-compliance
Lightning Source LLC
LaVergne TN
LVHW041300080426
835510LV00009B/811